THE CIVITAS CAPITALS OF ROMAN BRITAIN

THE CIVITAS CAPITALS
OF ROMAN BRITAIN

Papers given at a Conference held at the University of Leicester,
13-15 December 1963

Edited by

J. S. WACHER, B.SC., F.S.A.

LEICESTER UNIVERSITY PRESS
1966

DEDICATED
TO THE LATE
PROFESSOR SIR IAN RICHMOND

Printed in Great Britain by
ARMSTRONG-THORNLEY PRINTERS LIMITED
ANDOVER STREET, LEICESTER
for Leicester University Press

CONTENTS

LIST OF PLATES

LIST OF TEXT FIGURES

LIST OF ABBREVIATIONS

A.E.	*L'Année Epigraphique*
A.N.L.	*Archaeological News Letter*
Ann.	Tacitus, *Annales*
Antiq. J.	*Antiquaries Journal*
Arch.	*Archaeologia*
*Arch.Ael.*4	*Archaeologia Aeliana* (4th series)
Arch.Camb.	*Archaeologia Cambrensis*
Arch.Cant.	*Archaelogia Cantiana*
Arch. J.	*Archaeological Journal*
Bagendon	E. M. Clifford, *Bagendon, a Belgic Oppidum* (1961)
B.B.C.S.	*Bulletin of the Board of Celtic Studies*
Birm.Arch.Soc.	Birmingham Archaeological Society
B.G.	Julius Caesar, *de Bello Gallico*
Bull.Inst.Arch.	*Bulletin of the Institute of Archaeology,* University of London
Camulodunum	C. F. C. Hawkes & M. R. Hull, *Camulodunum.* Research Reports of the Society of Antiquaries of London, xiv (1947)
C.B.A.	Council for British Archaeology
C.I.L.	*Corpus Inscriptionum Latinarum*
Coll.rer.mem.	Solinus, *Collectanea rerum memorabilium*
D.A.J.	*Journal of the Derbyshire Archaeological & Natural History Society*
de Bell.Got.	Procopius, *de Bello Gothico*
Descr. Graec.	Pausanias, *Descriptio Graeciae*
E.E.	*Ephemeris Epigraphica*
E.H.R.	*English Historical Review*
Great Casterton I, II, III	*The Roman Town and Villa at Great Casterton, Rutland,* (ed.) P. Corder. I for 1951; II for 1952-3; III for 1954-8.
H.E.	Bede, *Historia Ecclesiastica*
Hist.	Tacitus, *Historiae*
I.L.S.	*Inscriptiones Latinae Selectae*
*J.B.A.A.*3	*Journal of the British Archaeological Association* (3rd series)
Jewry Wall	K. M. Kenyon, *Excavations at the Jewry Wall Site, Leicester.* Research Reports of the Society of Antiquaries of London, xv, (1948)
J.R.S.	*Journal of Roman Studies*
Lichfield & S. Staffs. A. & H. S.	Lichfield & South Staffordshire Archaeological and Historical Society
Med.Arch.	*Mediaeval Archaeology*
Nat.Hist. or *N.H.*	Pliny, *Natural History*
Not.Dig. (Occ.)	*Notitia Dignitatum (Occidentis)*
Norf.Arch.	*Norfolk Archaeology*
N.Staffs.J of F.S.	*North Staffordshire Journal of Field Studies*
O.S.	Ordnance Survey
P.Camb.Ant.S.	*Proceedings of the Cambridge Antiquarian Society*
P.Dev.A.E.S.	*Proceedings of the Devon Archaeological Exploration Society*
P.D.N.H.S.	*Proceedings of the Dorset Natural History and Archaeological Society*
P.H.F.C.	*Papers and Proceedings of the Hampshire Field Club and Archaeological Society*
P.Leeds Phil. & Lit.S.	*Proceedings of the Leeds Philosophical and Literary Society*
P.P.S.	*Proceedings of the Prehistoric Society*
P.S.A.	*Proceedings of the Society of Antiquaries*
P.S.A.L.	*Proceedings of the Society of Antiquaries of London*
P.S.A.S.	*Proceedings of the Society of Antiquaries of Scotland*

P.Som.A.N.H.S.	*Proceedings of the Somersetshire Archaeological and Natural History Society*
R.C.H.M.	*Royal Commission on Historical Monuments*
Rept.Res.Cttee.Wool. Club	*Report of the Research Committee of the Woolhope Club*
Roman Lincoln	*Roman Lincoln,* Report of the Lincolnshire Archaeological Research Committee (1955)
Roman Colchester	M. R. Hull, *Roman Colchester,* Research Reports of the Society of Antiquaries of London, xx (1958)
Sat.	Macrobius, *Saturnalia*
S.H.A.	*Scriptores Historiae Augustae*
Sx. or *Suss. A.C.*	*Sussex Archaeological Collections*
Sy.A.C.	*Surrey Archaeological Collections*
T.B.A.S.	*Transactions of the Birmingham Archaeological Society*
T.B.G.A.S.	*Transactions of the Bristol and Gloucestershire Archaeological Society*
T.L.A.S.	*The Leicestershire Archaeological and Historical Society Transactions*
T.Shrop.A.S.	*Transactions of the Shropshire Archaeological Society*
T.St.Albans A. & A.S.	*Transactions of the St. Albans Architectural and Archaeological Society*
T.Thoroton Soc.	*Transactions of the Thoroton Society*
T.W.A.S.	*Transactions of the Worcestershire Archaeological Society*
T.Wool. N.F.C.	*Transactions of the Woolhope Naturalist Field Club*
V.C.H.	*Victoria County History*
Verulamium	R. E. M. & T. V. Wheeler, *Verulamium: a Belgic and Two Roman Cities,* Research Reports of the Society of Antiquaries of London, xi (1936)
W.A.M.	*The Wiltshire Archaeological and Natural History Magazine*
Y.A.J.	*The Yorkshire Archaeological Journal*

BIBLIOGRAPHY

GENERAL.

Antiq. J., xviii, 42. F. Oswald considers possible military origins of certain cantonal capitals.

Arch. J., cxv, 49. G. Webster on the military advance under Ostorius Scapula, considers military origins and lists military equipment found on town sites.

Arch. J., cxii, 27. P. Corder on the dating of town walls and bastions. (For further information on bastions, see *The Roman Town and Villa at Great Casterton, Rutland*, iii, (Ed.) P. Corder.)

Arch. J., cxix, 103. J. Wacher on second-century earthwork defences.

Antiquity, xxxix, 57. M. Jarrett on town defences.

Antiquity, xx, 70. R. Goodchild on *fora*.

Arch., xc, 1. I. Richmond and O. Crawford on the Ravenna Cosmography.

Antiquity, xxxiv, 222; xxxv, 29. J. Mann and S. Frere on the status of towns.

Antiquity, xxxv, 316. Note by J. Mann on the administration of Roman Britain in the 4th century.

*J.B.A.A.*3, xvi, 14. J. Toynbee on early Christianity in Britain.

Arch. J., cxviii, 136. D. Dymond on bridges in Roman Britain. Includes summaries of evidence for some towns.

J. M. C. Toynbee: *Art in Roman Britain* (1964). Illustrates and describes many works of art from towns.

J. M. C. Toynbee: *Art in Britain under the Romans* (1964).

J. Liversidge: *Furniture in Roman Britain* (1955).

Antiquity and Survival, II, No. 4 (1958), 373. J. Liversidge on wall-plaster.

W. F. Grimes (Ed.): *Aspects of Archaeology in Britain and Beyond*. J. Myres on the *Adventus Saxonum*.

J.R.S., l, 21. J. Myres on *Pelagius and the end of Roman rule in Britain*.

Med. Arch., v, 1. G. Dunning and S. Hawkes on early Saxon metalwork. (See also *Bericht der Römisch-Germanischen Kommission*, 1962-3, p. 156.)

ALDBOROUGH. (*Isurium Brigantum*)

H. Ecroyd Smith: *Reliquiae Isurianae* (1852).

Lady Lawson-Tancred: *Guide Book to the Antiquities of Aldborough and Boroughbridge* (3rd Ed. 1948).

J.R.S., xiv, 221. North defences near gate.

Y.A.J., xl, 1. Excavations 1934-8. Mainly defences, including bastions and north gate.

J.R.S., li, 169. West defences.

BROUGH-ON-HUMBER. (*Petuaria*)

Antiq. J., xviii, 262. North Ferriby Belgic site.

Hull Museum Publications, no. 212, p. 237. North Ferriby Belgic site.

A. F. Norman: *The Romans in East Yorkshire* (1960).

M. K. Kitson Clarke: *Gazetteer of Roman Remains in East Yorkshire* (1935), 72-3.

P. Corder and T. Romans: *Excavations at Brough-on-Humber*, I (1934), East defences.

    Excavations at Brough-on-Humber, II (1935). East defences.

    Excavations at Brough-on-Humber, III (1936), East defences: gate. Flavian fort.

    Excavations at Brough-on-Humber, IV (1937), East defences: bastions. Flavian fort. Internal buildings (II-VI) and street.

    Excavations at Brough-on-Humber, V (1938), East defences: bastions. Flavian fort. Internal buildings (I). Theatre inscription.

*J.B.A.A.*3, vii, 1. Petuaria to 1942. Inscriptions, coin list, and Samian stamps.

Antiq. J., xviii, 68. Burial with sceptres.

Antiq. J., xl, 58. Excavation at Brough House 1958. North gate; north and west defences; internal buildings and streets. Flavian fort.

J.R.S., l, 220. Excavations at Grassdale 1959. Defences at south-east corner.

J.R.S.. li, 167. Excavations at Manor House 1960. Internal buildings and streets.

J.R.S., lii, 165. Excavations High Street sewer trench 1961. West defences. Flavian fort. Up-to-date plans.

CAERWENT. (*Venta Silurum*)

Carnuntina (Kongress der Alterumsforcher 1955) 1956, 100. General account.

Arch. Camb. (Centenary volume 1946). "*A Hundred Years of Welsh Archaeology,*" p. 105. A. Fox on Caerwent in the early Christian period.

Arch., xxxvi, 418. Excavations 1855. Baths, mosaics, summary to date.

Arch., lvii, 295. Excavations 1899-1900 in south-west corner.

Arch., lviii, 119, 391. Excavations 1901-2. Internal buildings. Painted wall-plaster.

Arch., lix, 87, 289. Excavations 1903-4. North, south gates; amphitheatre; Caerwent "stone", internal buildings; *mansio*.

Arch., lx, 111, 451. Excavations 1905-6. South gate; defences; internal buildings; painted plaster.

Arch., lxi. 565. Excavations 1907 and 1909. Forum and basilica; internal buildings.

Arch., lxii, 1, 405. Excavations 1908-10. Temples by forum; internal buildings; shops; streets; east gate.

Arch., lxiv, 437. Excavations 1911-12. Circular temple; internal buildings; streets.

Arch., lxxx, 229. Excavations 1925. South gate and defences; bath house; internal buildings (XXIV-XXVII-XXVIII).

B.B.C.S., xiv, 242. Coin list from 1925 excavations (*cf.* above).

B.B.C.S., xv, 159. Forum, basilica, and bath-house summary.

Antiq. J., xxxviii, 4n. Reassessment of date of earthwork defences.

CAISTOR ST. EDMUND. (*Venta Icenorum*)

Arch. J., cvi, 62. Summary of excavations 1929-35, and references to D. Atkinson's notes in *J.R.S.*

R. R. Clarke: *East Anglia* (1960).

Norf. Arch., xxx, 146. Summary to 1952.

J.R.S., xli, 132. External masonry structure.

J.R.S., xlvii, 211. External masonry structure—probably temple.

J.R.S., li, 132. Aerial photograph of early defensive circuit.

CANTERBURY. (*Durovernum Cantiacorum*)

S. S. Frere: *Roman Canterbury* No. 1. (1947).

S. S. Frere: *Roman Canterbury* (1960).

A. Williams: *Roman Canterbury*, No. 2. Excavations 1944. St George's Street.

A. Williams: *Roman Canterbury*, No. 3. Excavations 1945. Burgate and Watling Street.

A. Williams and S. S. Frere: *Roman Canterbury*, No. 4. Excavations 1945-6. Butchery Lane building.

F. Jenkins: *Roman Canterbury*, No. 5. Excavations 1946-8 in Burgate.

Arch., xliii, 151. Pillbrow's findings during main sewage scheme in 1867.

Arch. Cant., lxviii, 101. Excavations 1946. Rose Lane sites.

Antiquity, xxiii, 153. Summary of excavations to 1949.

Antiq. J., xxxvi, 40. Tile and pottery kilns at St Stephen's.

J.R.S., xxxviii, 96. St George Street baths (1947).

J.R.S., xxxix, 110. Rose Lane buildings (1948). Town wall.

J.R.S., xl, 113. St George's Street buildings (1949). Street.

J.R.S., xli, 138. Theatre (1950). Burgate Street.

J.R.S., xlii, 102. Theatre (1951).

J.R.S., xliii. 127. Defences in Westgate Gardens; extra-mural settlement (1952).

J.R.S., xliv, 102. Riding Gate; Watling Street (1953).

J.R.S., xlv, 143. Riding Gate; defences in Burgate Lane (1954).

J.R.S., xlvi, 144. West gate; Castle (defences). Forum (1955).

J.R.S., xlvii, 225. Marlowe Car Park; theatre (1956).

J.R.S., xlviii, 149. Marlowe Car Park; theatre (1957).

J.R.S., xlix, 135. Burgate; forum area behind Fleur de Lys Hotel (1958).

J.R.S., l, 236. Further excavation on Butchery Lane building (1959).

J.R.S., li, 191. Bastion and defences in Dane John gardens; Saxon huts in Simon Langton school yard (1960).

Arch. Cant., lxxiv, 151. Tile and pottery kilns at Whitehall.

J.R.S., lii, 190. Worthgate noted in gas-trench.

J.R.S., liii, 158. Silver hoard from south-west defences.

CIRENCESTER. (*Corinium Dobunnorum*)

T.B.G.A.S., xiv, 221. Leland's visit described.

General information : S. Rudder : *A New History of Gloucestershire* (1779), p. 343.

K. J. Beecham : *History of Cirencester* (1886).

W. St C. Baddeley : *History of Cirencester* (1924).

J. Buckman and C. H. Newmarch : *Remains of Roman Art in Cirencester* (1850). Dyer Street and Barton pavements and general descriptions.

Arch., lxix, 161. Digest up to 1917 by Haverfield. Table of find spots and mosaics, inscriptions, and sculpture.

J.B.A.A., xxv, 106. Early excavations at the amphitheatre in 1848.

T.B.G.A.S., xxi, 70. ⎫
P.S.A., xvii, 201.   ⎬ Excavations on the basilica in 1897-8.

T.B.G.A.S., xvi, 229. Columns found in the Leauses.

T.B.G.A.S., xvii, 12. Street in Ashcroft.

P.S.A., xviii, 177. Ashcroft sculptures.

T.B.G.A.S., lxvii, 383. Excavations at Victoria Road sawmills in 1947.

T.B.G.A.S., lxx, 51. Date of Barton Pavement.

T.B.G.A.S., lxxv, 203. Street in Querns House garden.

T.B.G.A.S., lxxvi, 21. Christian cryptogram.

T.B.G.A.S., lxxviii, 44. Dyer Court excavations in 1958. Ermine Street and flanking buildings.

T.B.G.A.S., lxxxi, 41. Painted wall-plaster from Dyer Court excavations.

J.R.S., xlii, 98. Mosaic found on Mycalex site.

J.R.S., xlix, 127. Bingham Hall gardens and Health Clinic sites.

Antiq. J., xxxvii, 206. Excavations in Watermoor, 1952. Defences at east corner.

Antiq. J., xli, 63. Excavations in Abbey grounds, 1960. Verulamium Gate and north-east defences.

Antiq. J., xlii, 1. Excavations in The Avenue 1961. Early fort; basilica, market, shops in insula V; street grid; building XXI, 1.

Antiq. J., xlii, 160. Excavations in Parsonage Field, 1959; building IV, 1.

Antiq. J., xliii, 17. Excavations, 1962. Amphitheatre; south-east defences; insulae XI, XVIII, XXIII, XXVII; streets.

Antiq. J., xliv, 9. Excavations, 1963. Amphitheatre; south-west defences; forum; insulae IV, XXII; streets.

Antiq. J., xlv, 97. Excavations 1964. Fort; insulae VI, XIII, XXV, XXVIII; streets.

Also of interest :

E. M. Clifford : *Bagendon : a Belgic Oppidum* (1961).

CHICHESTER. (*Noviomagus Regnensium*)

Sx.A.C., lxxvi, 135. Recent finds to 1933-4.

Sx.A.C., xc, 164. Excavations 1947-50. Defences; internal sites.

Sx.A.C., xciv, 100. Beginnings of Roman Chichester (A. E. Wilson).

Sx.A.C., c, 73. Excavations 1958-60. Defences; buildings in North Street.

J.R.S., liii, 151. Excavations 1962, on a number of sites. Forum area; bath-house; streets.

DORCHESTER. (*Durnovaria*)

P.D.N.H.S., xxix, 256.   ⎫
P.D.N.H.S., xxx, 217.   ⎪
P.D.N.H.S., xxxi, 230.   ⎬ Excavations, 1908-13, on the amphitheatre, Maumbury rings.
P.D.N.H.S., xxxiv, 81.   ⎪
P.D.N.H.S., xxxv, 88.   ⎭

P.D.N.H.S., lix, 1. ⎫
P.D.N.H.S., lx, 51. ⎬ Excavations, 1937-8, on Colliton Park buildings.

P.D.N.H.S., lxxv, 72. Excavations on defences, 1951.

P.D.N.H.S., lxxvii, 128. Excavations on defences, 1955.

Antiq. J., xx, 435. The aqueduct excavations in 1939.

J.R.S., lii, 185. Excavations 1961 in Colliton Park. First-century chalk-pit; internal buildings.

J.R.S., liii, 148. Excavations 1962 in Colliton Park. Internal buildings.

Also of interest :

R. E. M. Wheeler : *Maiden Castle* (Soc. of Antiq. Res. Report No. 12).

EXETER. (*Isca Dumnoniorum*)

R. G. Goodchild: *Roman Exeter* (1946).
A. Fox: *Roman Exeter* (1952). Excavations 1945-7. Includes description of defences; early buildings and possible forum in South Street area.
J.R.S., l, 230. Excavations in Gaumont Cinema Car Park in 1959.
J.R.S., lii, 184. Excavations on south defences in 1961.

ILCHESTER. (*Lindinis*)

P.Som.A.& N.H.S., xcvi, 188. The Roman name of Ilchester (C. E. Stevens).
Arch. J., cvii, 94. Brief note on town.
J.R.S., xxxix, 108; xl, 110. Excavations 1948-9 on defences.

LEICESTER. (*Ratae Coritanorum*)

Arch. J., lxxv, 7. Survey by Haverfield to 1918, with find spots and references.
K. M. Kenyon: *The Jewry Wall* (1948). Excavations 1936-9 on the baths and Raw Dykes aqueduct.
T.L.A.S., xxviii, 17. Summary 1939-51.
T.L.A.S., xxix, 15. Excavations 1952 on north defences. Note on Thurmaston milestone.
J.R.S., xlix, 113. Excavations 1958 on buildings in Blue Boar Lane. Decorated wall plaster; basilican market; north defences.
J.R.S., li, 175. Excavations 1960 in Blackfriars area.
J.R.S., lii, 172. Excavations 1961 in Gt Central Street. Probably north wing of forum.
J.R.S., liii, 134. Excavations 1962 in central area. Internal buildings and street plan.

SILCHESTER. (*Calleva Atrebatum*)

T. May: *The Pottery Found at Silchester* (1916).
G. C. Boon: *Roman Silchester* (1957).
Arch., xl, 403. Excavations 1864. Internal buildings.
Arch., xlvi, 329. Excavations 1865-7. Internal buildings; forum; basilica; east, south gates.
Arch., l, 263. Excavations 1886. Internal buildings; *mansio* baths.
Arch., lii, 733. Excavations 1891. Internal buildings; temples near east gate; north, south, west gates.
Arch., liii, 539. Excavations 1892. Forum; basilica; surroundings, including church.
Arch., liv, 439. Excavations 1894. Internal buildings; dyeing workshops (?).
Arch., lv, 215, 409. Excavations 1895-6. Internal buildings; force-pump; west postern gate.
Arch., lvi, 103, 229. Excavations 1897-8. Internal buildings; wine barrels.
Arch., lvii, 113, 229. Excavations 1899-1900. Internal buildings; silver refinery.
Arch., lviii, 17, 413. Excavations 1901-2. Internal buildings; water-gate.
Arch., lix, 333. Excavations 1903. Internal buildings; baths.
Arch., lx, 149, 431. Excavations 1905-6. Internal buildings; tanning troughs (?).
Arch., lxi, 199, 473. Excavations 1907-8. Internal buildings; "Calleva" inscription; east, west gates.
Arch., lxii, 317. Excavations 1909. Defences.
Antiquity, xxii, 172. Early plan and town houses.
Arch., xcii, 121. Excavations 1938-9. Defences; postern gate; street plan.
P.H.F.C., xxi, 9. Excavations 1954-7. Inner earthwork.
Med. Arch., iii, 79. Dark-age finds.
J.R.S., lii, 185. Excavations 1961. Christian church re-excavated.

VERULAMIUM.

R. E. M. & T. V. Wheeler: *Verulamium: a Belgic and two Roman Cities* (1936). Excavations 1930-4. Defences; gates; insulae I-X.
Arch., lxxxiv, 213. Excavations 1933-4 on the theatre.
Antiq. J., xvii, 28. Excavations 1934 on the temple in insula XVI and north-east corner of forum; internal buildings.
Arch., xc, 81. Excavations 1938 on the market hall in insula XVII.
T.St.Albans A. & A.S. (1953), 20. Excavations 1949 on south-west side of the forum and forum temples.

VERULAMIUM (*continued*).

Antiq. J., xxxvi, 1. Excavations 1955. First-century defences; town wall on south-west side; buildings in insulae XX – XXII.

Antiq. J., xxxvii, 1. Excavations 1956. Belgic mint; town wall on north-east; ditch beneath forum; north-west side of forum; basilica inscription; river bank; buildings in insulae XX, XXII, XXVII.

Antiq. J., xxxviii, 1. Excavations 1957. Extra-mural buildings; buildings in insulae VII, XIV, XXVII, XXVIII.

Antiq. J., xxxix, 1. Excavations 1958. Buildings in insulae XIV, XXVIII; painted ceiling.

Antiq. J., xl, 1. Excavations 1959. First-century defences; town wall; theatre; buildings in insulae XIV, XVIII, XXI, XXVI, XXVIII.

Antiq. J., xli, 72. Excavations 1960. Claudian fort? Buildings in insulae XIV, XIX, XXI, XXVII, XXVIII.

Antiq. J., xlii, 148. Excavations 1961. Northern triumphal arch; first-century town defences; town wall on north-east side; insula XVIII.

T. St. Albans A. & A. S., (1961), 36. Belgic mint; street.

Antiquity, xxxviii, 103. Summary to 1964.

Bull. Inst. Arch., iv, 69. Summary to 1964.

WINCHESTER. (*Venta Belgarum*)

P.H.F.C., xviii, 62, 315. Excavations 1951, 1953, in Middle Brook Street.

P.H.F.C., xix, 1. Excavations 1954 in St George's Street and Middle Brook Street.

P.H.F.C., xxii, 51. Excavations 1951-60 on defences.

Arch. J., cxix, 150. Excavations 1961 in Cathedral Car Park.

Antiq. J., xliv, 188. Excavations 1962-3.

WROXETER. (*Viroconium Cornoviorum*)

T. Wright: *Viroconium: An account of the ancient Roman city of Wroxeter* (1872).

(Ed.) I. Ll. Foster and L. Alcock: *Culture and Environment* (1963), p. 251. I. Richmond on the Cornovii.

J. P. Bushe-Fox: *Society of Antiquaries Research Reports* I, II, IV. Excavations on internal buildings in 1912-14.

D. Atkinson: *Excavations at Wroxeter* 1923-7. Defences; forum and basilica; early baths.

Arch., lxxxviii, 175. Excavations 1936-7. Defences; later baths.

J.R.S., xliii, 81, 84, 88. Aerial photographs.

J.R.S., xlv, 88. Aerial photograph of possible legionary fortress.

T.B.A.S., lxix, 54. Auxiliary fort.

J.R.S., xliii, 118.
J.R.S., xliv, 93.
J.R.S., xlix, 112. } 1953 – present day: excavations on bath-building.
J.R.S., l, 222.
J.R.S., li, 173.
J.R.S., lii, 169.

T.B.A.S., lxxviii, 27. Defences reconsidered.

T. Shrop. A.S., xlvii, 79. Aqueduct.

T. Shrop. A.S., lvi, 133. Aqueduct.

T. Shrop. A.S., lvii, 112. Summary to 1964.

EDITOR'S NOTE

THE conference on Romano-British Cantonal Capitals, which was held at Leicester University in December 1963, was the outcome of a joint discussion between Mr David Clarke, then Keeper of Antiquities at the City Museum, and the Editor. The idea of the conference, once developed, was put to the University's Department of Adult Education, who agreed to undertake its organization. The Editor would like to place on record his gratitude to the members of that Department, notably Mr D. J. Rice, Warden, and Mr H. N. Jeffery, then Bursar of Vaughan College, for undertaking the heavy administrative duties involved; also to Mr J. Crompton, Warden of Digby Hall, and his staff, for the excellent accommodation they provided.

Between 270 and 280 people attended the Conference, and heard a series of short papers describing recent discoveries in certain cantonal capitals: — *Exeter* by Lady Fox; *Chichester* by John Holmes; *Silchester* by G. C. Boon; *Canterbury* by Professor S. S. Frere; *Dorchester* by R. A. H. Farrar; *Winchester* by Martin Biddle; *Leicester* by M. G. Hebditch; and *Wroxeter* by Dr G. Webster. Six longer papers concerned with broader aspects of the subject were also given, together with an introductory talk by Professor Sir Ian Richmond, and a final summing-up by A. L. F. Rivet.

It was decided after the conference had taken place, that a printed version would be valuable, not only to those who came but also to those who were unable to attend. But it was also decided to omit, with one exception, the short papers dealing with individual towns, since most of the material produced was ephemeral in character, and would be published independently. The exception to this rule was Lady Fox's paper on *Exeter,* reproduced in this volume in full as a rebuttal to Dr Webster's suggestions that the civilian town of Exeter was preceded by a fort, although excavations have since shown that Dr Webster was probably right in his assumption (*cf.* pp. 45, n.62 and 51, n.9).

The final form of this volume therefore includes the six main papers and Roman Exeter together with the introduction and summing-up. In addition, there is a contribution by Dr J. K. St Joseph, who was unable to accept the invitation to give a paper at the conference itself. A bibliography covering all Romano-British cantonal capitals has also been added.

The Editor also wishes to acknowledge with much gratitude the generous help given in the publication of this book by the staff of Leicester University Press and Professor J. Simmons, Mr A. L. F. Rivet, and Mrs A. Wacher who took responsibility for the later stages of the editorial work.

INTRODUCTORY
by
Professor Sir Ian Richmond

"OF THE making of books there is no end"; and this can apply to conferences. There is, however, no doubt that such gatherings are often the means of attracting a new public to the subject and to the particular issue discussed, and so it proved at Leicester. For the hall was filled not only by familiar figures but by new ones, and the lectures were followed with keen attention. Another merit of the conference was the taking of stock and the setting of new objectives which emerged. Applied to the fifteen cantonal capitals of Roman Britain this process came to mean that out of fifteen about half a dozen might be considered tolerably well known, and this prompted the questions of how much and just what ought to be asked of the others. This is not merely a matter of not knowing their plans in detail: it is more often an ignorance of even the most general terms of their history.

Environmental study of the cantonal capitals is also much needed, since interest in their development as towns often tends to eclipse their importance as heads of districts. So little is known as to how their territory was organized or even what were the minor administrative centres, controlling the *pagi,* within it. Indeed such an inquiry would provide an antidote to the tendency which has been so marked in this generation, to turn so-called villages into homesteads. Salutary though this process has been, the fact remains that there were within each canton numerous sites which could correctly be described as villages: and yet in the majority of such places literally nothing, or virtually nothing, is known of either the sites or their inhabitants. A second element of great importance in the cantonal area is the large estate. The great land-owners represent the aristocracy of the tribe, whose words and policy determined what happened in the council of the cantonal capital. In this field also, despite some knowledge of isolated instances, there remains almost everything to do. When it comes to estimating the social composition of the canton in terms of civilization, it is essential to know not only how many large estates existed, but what kind of people lived in them and what level of culture they had reached. This has much to do with the cantonal capital itself, for it raises the question how many of the *decuriones,* who were in effect the great land-owners, lived in the tribal capital or how many in the countryside which it governed. In the tribe of the Silures, unless the number of decurions was extraordinarily few, it seems certain that many were not living in the capital town at all. On the other hand, it has been observed that at Wroxeter (Viroconium Cornoviorum) a large number would appear to have been living in the town. This kind of information, however, raises important points in tribal policy and tribal social life. It must be asked whether the decurions lived in the capital because they enjoyed the opportunity to form a group of cultivated society, or because, whatever their level of civilization, they felt more comfortable and safer behind the defences of the town. The town itself may supply many details which will answer this question in part. The town-plan, the public buildings, the houses and the shops will all have their contribution to make. But the picture must be completed by evidence from the countryside and the whole question of tribal civilization broadens into a theme which embraces not merely the town but the countryside of which the town is a reflection. This matter is likely to occupy Romano-British studies for at least a generation.

Town defences pose a more limited problem, yet one which still demands that definition which comes only from hard facts. Not a single town in Roman Britain has yet yielded a gateway inscription commemorating the erection of the defences, though these must once have existed just as surely as actual examples show them to have existed on the Continent. When the difficulties are considered of such evidence as must today be used to date the town-defences of Britain, it becomes hard to believe that most must once have been dated firmly by a monumental inscription. As it is, present evidence points, with a striking consensus of estimation, to a date usually classified as the close of the second century or the beginning of the third. But this is virtually meaningless in relation to the history of the province, and still more so in relation to the history of the towns themselves, since it cannot be linked with any of the hard facts of history known from other sources. The work is tedious, as all those who have cut sections through town defences know: and so often the evidence is itself insufficiently secure, since it will have represented results from one section only.

The organization of town defences raises the no less important and interesting question as to how they were normally manned or guarded. It remains unknown whether there was a cantonal militia to look after them, or whether the task was divided among the burghers or their guilds. Not a single relevant inscription exists, nor does any other information throw light upon the matter. Yet it is no unimportant question, since it has such a significant bearing upon how the towns might have been organized when it came to fending for themselves after A.D. 410. A systematic tradition of wall-defence would have enabled them to hold out as organized communities without the dangerously fatal hiring of mercenaries, so often suicidal in its effect. Even at Silchester, however, where knowledge of the plan of the buildings in masonry may be claimed as reasonably complete, no building on the plan emerges as candidate for the headquarters of a militia or comparable organization.

Within the towns much remains to be done in the matter of gauging their degree of civilization. Recent records are promising, and it is striking how much has been learnt from the wall-plaster recovered and reconstructed at Verulamium. The process is cumulative and it can be seen that wall-plaster is beginning to take its proper place alongside the much less vulnerable and more easily preserved mosaic pavement. It would already appear that in the wall-plaster there is a no less close connexion with the current patterns of the Roman world at large than in mosaics. At present the mosaics indeed would seem to exhibit more individuality, but this may well be an impression which further material will modify.

Another profitable field of inquiry lies in a study of the small bronzes from the British cantonal capitals. No such study as yet exists and an exhibition of representative examples recently assembled at the Goldsmiths' Hall held qualitative surprises. This, however, was a minute proportion of the existing material, which is seen to have its own specially vivid contribution to make to the history of cantonal civilization. A well-published Corpus of these bronzes is a real need, and one in the fulfilment of which our Continental colleagues can put us to shame. Into this sphere, even more than into the craft of wall-painting or mosaic, the native craftsman enters alongside the Roman. Each manifests his own style, but there are also fusions and occasions when the native artist emerges uncontaminated and triumphant. Here form enables us to get nearest to the spoken word and must indeed do duty for it.

How rich, on the other hand, and how suggestive is the information which has been furnished by Professor Kenneth Jackson's great work on *Language and History in Early Britain*. Those who will read it with discretion learn from it what they never knew before, just what kind of Latin was used and spoken by the folk of the cantonal capitals. At best it was schoolroom Latin, in the sense of being polished and careful speech. It did not degenerate into the low Latin or colloquial language which in Gaul was in due time to turn into French. Not only did this never happen in Britain, but none of the preliminary symptoms appears. This important and interesting fact arises from the class of people who were using the speech. They represented the top level of cantonal society, who had learnt their Latin carefully and rigidly in the schoolroom. An explanation is thus forthcoming for the governor Agricola's belief that the Britons might do better in elocution and rhetoric than the Gauls, no doubt because it was a little more difficult for them and they took trouble about it: at least Agricola refers to their native power of mind. He did not indeed recognize it as a national characteristic, like the willingness to pay taxes so long as these were fair. Yet the characteristic does remain in the Briton of today, that he will be shy of speaking in a foreign language until he thinks he can use it effectively and with reasonable accuracy. The trait can be seen to have come right through to modern days. The cantonal life is indeed reflected in the remarkable list compiled by Professor Jackson of loan-words taken from Latin into Welsh. Many are connected with structural terms and with public buildings, many with housekeeping in the sense of butler's work and the like, many again with the products of agriculture and with tools: words such as the bailiff might use. This exactly reflects the upper level of cantonal life or of the people who ran the community, the towns-folk, the estate owners, or their agents. What of the rest? In their sphere Professor Jackson makes it clear that Celtic was freely used and spoken. It becomes evident, for example, that when in the cantonal court of justice a local law case was pleaded it must usually have been pleaded in Celtic. When, on the other hand, the case concerned a Roman citizen and a Celt the proceedings might have been in Latin, but the Celt would require an interpreter, and inter-preters were not uncommon in the ancient world.

The linguistic discoveries of Professor Jackson explain many points about cantonal society which have remained until now obscure. It becomes clear why the veneer of culture was in a sense so thin, an upper crust very easily shattered and dispersed. It helps to explain why events in Britain after the breakdown of the central government went their own particular way and not that which was taken in Gaul. Latin speech did not continue in Britain because, as can now be seen, it was never part of the British heritage as a whole, and, when the upper classes perished, it died with them. The words which went on and passed into Welsh were those of the estate owners: for the land and its use endured, since estates last in one fashion or another, whoever may own them, and whatever language the owner may speak; while with the estates goes their apparatus, for which the names survived in the mouths of the servants and workers.

THE TOWNS OF ROMAN BRITAIN

THE CONTRIBUTION OF AERIAL RECONNAISSANCE

by

J. K. St Joseph

ROMAN towns from the very extent and complexity of their structure offer unusually varied opportunities for study from the air. In the Middle East and in Mediterranean lands upstanding remains so considerable may survive that architectural studies assume first importance. Nevertheless an air photograph offers a possibility of presenting from a single view-point an entire town often with great advantage to those who would study the choice of site, the development of a town-plan, or the relationship of the principal buildings to one another.[1] Although in many provinces of the Empire Roman levels are buried deep below medieval and modern towns which occupy the same site, much may still be learnt from the air about Roman town-planning, since ancient town-walls, streets, and not infrequently large buildings have often determined the position of modern features by which they are, indeed, reflected. There also exist Roman towns that have not been occupied by settlements of later date. A covering of soil and vegetation hides all, so that no architectural remains are visible and earthworks alone mark the site. These conditions may actually favour research by observation from the air, particularly in north-west Europe where the prevailing climate and vegetation offer unexpected opportunities for the study of such towns, even though little may be seen by an observer on the ground.

In Britain there are towns where Roman defences or streets may still be discerned in an aerial photograph, even though the Roman levels lie beneath remains of later ages, as the town has developed over the centuries: Colchester, Gloucester, Lincoln, York, and Chichester are examples. But the abundant opportunities for the study in Britain of Roman towns comparatively unencumbered by later features are not always realized. Of towns which are large in size by the standards of the province, St Albans, and the cantonal capitals of Wroxeter and Silchester, as well as the rather smaller Caistor-by-Norwich present almost their whole extent free for observation, while restricted areas within Caerwent, Aldborough, and, at least until recently, in Cirencester, remain open ground. Interesting comparisons may be made between these towns and those of smaller size, of which there are rather more examples unencumbered by later structures and available for study from the air: Chesterton (Water Newton), Irchester, Mildenhall (Wilts.), Kenchester, Great Chesterford, Weston under Penyard, Alchester (Oxon.), Great Casterton, Ancaster, and Catterick, all forty acres or less in extent. Of road-side settlements which developed in response to differing needs, as by growth of buildings round a *mansio*, Brough on Fosse, Thorpe, Chesterton on Fosse, Dorn,

Camerton, Mancetter, Stretton, Alfoldean, Hardham, and Wanborough lie on ground that is wholly or largely free of modern structures. So far as the evidence goes the simplest materials, wood, clay, wattle, and thatch were used for most of the buildings at these settlements, yet a number are listed in Roman Itineraries and their Latinized names are known.[2] At all these places the opportunities open to an aerial observer vary from year to year, and at towns of larger size, even in any given year, from one part of the area to another, as different crops are brought by agricultural rotation to each field in turn.

Many of these towns have now been kept under observation for nearly twenty years, in flights sponsored by the Committee for Aerial Photography of the University of Cambridge. This period is long enough to assess the value of aerial research, even allowing for limitations imposed by unfavourable weather, unresponsive vegetation, and infertile soils, while comparison between one site and another is facilitated by having a small collection of photographs reproduced together as illustrations to a single article. What of the results?

At Wroxeter,[3] in area the fourth largest town in the province, the Forum and a small area near it has already been excavated. Air photographs reveal (Plate I) some 70 acres of the town-plan,[4] not only streets but public and private buildings, including temples, a market, and other large buildings comprising long rows of rooms and corridors which appear clearly marked in the growing crops. Of private buildings, there are large town-houses with courtyards, corridors, and ranges of rooms : other structures may be tentatively identified as shops and store-houses. The largest and most elaborate buildings lie around the Forum and 'baths', as if buildings of some architectural quality were grouped in this quarter of the town. Photographs of this kind afford us a new basis for assessing the life and economy of a cantonal capital, yielding a plan matched in point of completeness only by that recorded by excavation at Silchester. The street-plan of the northern half of Wroxeter presents unexplained eccentricities which raise the question whether the extent of the town was envisaged at the start on a rather ample scale, and that in some sectors the street-system grew piecemeal as development proceeded.

At such a large site, photography repeated annually may be expected to bring new information about the history of the whole area. Outside the town both to south and north, crop marks reveal enclosures of a kind often associated with Romano-British farmsteads. Further information about rural settlement in the territory of the Cornovii is greatly to be desired. Military remains have also come to light, comprising so far a $5\frac{1}{2}$ acre auxiliary fort lying a quarter of a mile outside the town to the south,[5] two temporary camps, to judge from the incomplete outlines at present known, and a ditch-system of military type[6] underlying buildings of the town itself. In the last twenty years' reconnaissance of Wroxeter, it is interesting to note that buildings within the town presented exceptionally clear crop marks in 1948, 1949, and 1950 when the information obtained far exceeded the yield of the remaining 17 years together. On the other hand, the clearest rendering in terms of crop marks of long sectors of the north-east defences was seen in 1951 and 1955. Evidently crops make a very individual response to buried features, while an exceptionally favourable conjunction of crops, weather and soil may occur once in a decade or more.

Silchester, in Hampshire, the tribal capital of the Atrebates, was explored between 1890 and 1909, in one of the longest series of campaigns of excavation ever conducted in Britain at a single site.[7] Such extensive exploration of a large Roman town is today hardly in question, and indeed, the best deployment of resources now involves the selection with the aid of air photography of points where significant features in a town can be studied, so that comparatively small areas can be examined by digging. The apparent completeness of the plan of Silchester is itself deceptive. Are the large blank areas in Insulae I, X, XI, XXIIa, and XXIII really so devoid of buildings as to give the impression that much of this town was never fully built up? Under favourable conditions, not only do the buildings at Silchester promote crop marks (Plate II), but even the excavators' exploratory trenches dug sixty years ago across areas that were never completely stripped have been seen to cause difference in growth of crops. During the last twenty years the whole of the area of the town save the two fields nearest the parish church, overlying Insulae V-VI, XXVIII-XXXII, XXXIV, has been photographed when the ground was under cereal crops. The majority of the large excavated buildings have been seen again in this way, and in addition, a number of stone buildings that have apparently escaped attention until now. These are of the greatest interest for they should yield the stratified levels from which the history of the town may yet be determined. Nor will stone have been the only building material in use : timber structures also are surely to be looked for, and if they do not prove too difficult to trace in the gravel soil of Silchester a somewhat different plan may eventually emerge.

At Silchester, too, an unexpectedly complicated sequence in the defences has come to light. It is well known that the polygonal earthen rampart, to which a stone wall was later added, represents a reduction of the fortified area in the late second century : the grid of streets going with an outer circuit of earthwork defences. The metalling of the streets inside the polygonal wall often promotes crop marks,[8] which may even reveal such details as the existence of a gutter or drain down the centre of a street. That part of the grid that lies outside the wall, if visible at all, is only seen under conditions of drought, and even then as very faint marks. It may be supposed that this part of the system had a comparatively short life, and never acquired the thick layers of metalling of the streets permanently within the town. Moreover, air photography has revealed yet a third system of defences, namely a buried ditch that underlies both the street-grid and the polygonal defensive circuit already mentioned. This, an earlier Silchester than any yet known, has good claim to be identified as the Belgic *oppidum*.

A well-known photograph taken from an aircraft of the Royal Air Force during the summer drought of 1928 showed the whole street-plan and many of the buildings of Caistor-by-Norwich,[9] thus demonstrating for the first time how much knowledge might be gained from the application of this method of research to Romano-British towns. How rare is the chance of obtaining such a result was hardly appreciated at the time, and indeed it was not until September 1940 that comparable material again came to hand in Britain. Vertical photographs of St Albans then taken[10] show much of the southern half of the Roman town which lies in a public park.

The most important point to emerge from recent photography (Plate III) of Caistor concerns the plan of the defences. Photographs demonstrate beyond doubt that this town, the cantonal capital of the Iceni, was at some unknown date reduced in size by nearly a quarter.[11] The north-to-south members of the grid of streets can be seen continuing southwards outside the line of visible defences. They are linked by an east-to-west street: beyond is a space wide enough for a rampart, and then the lines of two ditches, which may be presumed to mark the early limit of the town. Whenever excavation is resumed at Caistor, the photographs show where digging could be undertaken to settle the important question of the date of this reduction.

At St Albans, the photographs of 1940, already mentioned, have proved of value in the planning of subsequent excavations. In the north-western half of the town, conditions do not ordinarily favour the formation of crop marks. Occasional buildings have come to light in the insulae south-west of the theatre, but the most interesting new information bears on the development of the town defences. The crops in fields north of Bluehouse Hill have revealed a buried ditch, in all probability part of the same Claudian defensive circuit that has been traced by excavation further to the south-east,[12] and of which the west angle is known from a magnetometer survey. Photographs show that Watling Street makes a very slight bend to the west at a point within the field north-east of Gorhambury Drive half-way between the theatre and the north-west gate in the later defences. Crop marks on the site of the road just south of this bend have prompted excavations showing the marks to be caused by the foundations of a monumental arch,[13] astride the road just within the line of the Claudian defences. The bend would be explained by the need for the road-engineers to take account of a gateway-position fixed even before the road was consolidated.

Of the smaller towns, Alchester (Oxon),[14] some 25 acres in extent, seems to have had a regular grid of streets though not all the plan is known with certainty, while at Alcester (Warwickshire), three parallel streets appear in dry summers in fields south of the modern town. Too little of the settlement remains free of later buildings for effective study from the air. At Mildenhall,[15] in Wiltshire, a town of about 19 acres, where air reconnaissance has proved the existence of two defensive circuits,[16] the later comprising a massive stone wall with projecting bastions, the street-system so far as it is known seems to be a fairly regular grid.

PLATE I. WROXETER, Salop. Streets and many buildings including large houses are seen as crop marks in barley, in field 422, north-east of the baths.

PLATE II. SILCHESTER, Hampshire. The photograph includes most of Insula VII (foreground) and the whole of Insula IV. The Basilica, Forum, and a circular foundation of a temple may be distinguished together with other buildings.

PLATE III. CAISTOR-BY-NORWICH, Norfolk. This vertical photograph shows that the original street-grid is cut by visible defences on the south (foreground). Two parallel ditches there mark the position of an early defensive circuit. Scale 1 : 4,500.

PLATE IV. CHESTERTON, Hunts. The town is laid out on level ground between the flood-plain of the Nene (off the right-hand margin) and the Billing Brook, seen in the distance. The straight course of Ermine Street and the irregularly planned side-streets are clearly visible.

PLATE V. IRCHESTER, Northants. The town extended over the whole of the large field above the modern road, sloping gently towards the River Nene (in the distance). The obtuse angle in the west defences (left) is seen: the east town wall is marked by a row of widely spaced trees. Part of the irregular street-plan appears.

PLATE VI. THORPE, Notts. The rectangular walled town is set on a terrace above the flood-plain of the Trent. The polygonal ditched enclosure lies in the field to the right.

PLATE VII. BROUGH ON FOSSE, Notts. Vertical photograph showing to north-west (left) of the modern road a maze of pits and trenches cut across by two wide ditches. Scale 1:2,800.

These photographs are from the Cambridge University Collection. The copyright is reserved.

Here seven different stone buildings have been noted within the town : one is an elaborate house.

Chesterton (Water Newton), Kenchester, and Irchester have an irregular mesh of streets, lacking the systematic planning of the larger towns. At Chesterton,[17] in Huntingdonshire, the hexagonal area of 44 acres enclosed by the defences gives a misleading impression of careful planning. Ermine Street has here been laid out in a straight length of over six miles, passing through the site of the town, and undeviating even at the crossing of the Nene, 1,400 ft away. The line of the defences on the south-east and west sides seems to have been determined by the need to enclose land not liable to flooding : the position of the north-east defences which lie along the edge of the flood-plain, is particularly striking. Such considerations explain how it came about that Ermine Street enters the town somewhat to the south of the mid-point of the short south-east side, and leaves the town almost at the north angle, dividing the defended area into two unequal parts. The one other gate that is known lies in the long south-west side at a point where the line of the defences is staggered.

The defences of the town comprise a stone wall now seen by reason of the light-toned mass of debris that overlies whatever of the structure remains in place. In 1957 the line of the wall itself was visible as a crop mark along the southern part of the south-west side. A suggestion based upon photographs that there are small square bastions as at the neighbouring Great Casterton deserves to be tested by digging. The construction of the wall and of the clay bank behind it, has been ascribed to the second century on the evidence of a section near the south-west gate.[18] For two-thirds of the perimeter the extent of the built-up area is limited by the edge of the flood-plain, and, given the course of Ermine Street, no street-grid dividing the town into regular insulae of normal size is possible. In fact, Ermine Street forms the long axis of the town (Plate IV), and from this 'spine-road', side streets branch off obliquely, following for the most part gently curving courses : there is no question of careful planning here. Further branches serve the outer parts of the town with the result that the 'building plots' (insulae seems hardly the right term for them) are of irregular shape and size. Only in one place on the west are there two plots of approximately equal dimensions.

As to structures within the town, Artis' plan published in 1828[19] shows no less than 22 buildings, or parts of buildings. Air photographs confirm this picture: after fresh ploughing, patches of light-toned earth formed from the weathering of building debris may be seen widely scattered over the whole area. When conditions are favourable for the development of crop marks, the impression gained is that substantial buildings in stone lie not far below the surface in many of the building-plots. Near the centre of the town, and on the south side of Ermine Street, to which it is set obliquely, is a rectangular building with sides that may be estimated as 100 ft or more in length. Rooms seem to be ranged round a courtyard : it would be interesting to know if this were a *mansio*. Of other buildings, only outlines appear for the most part : the dozen that can clearly be identified are rectangular in shape; and as to size, an estimate of 20 ft by 40 ft or 25 ft by 50 ft is unlikely to be far wrong. The impression gained is that the frontages of Ermine Street at least in the northern half of the town, were closely built up, with structures mostly set end-on to the more valuable street frontage : elsewhere the alignment of buildings seems haphazard.

Any consideration of the plan of Chesterton, and in particular the character of its buildings, must take into account the situation of the town, in the centre of the Castor pottery industry. Other buildings are known from excavation and from aerial photography to occur outside the town, for example, beside Ermine Street to the south,[20] quite apart from the numerous potters' kilns. Not only should store-houses on an appropriate scale be postulated, but the question arises where lay the dwellings of these who worked the potteries? Nothing is known in detail of the organisation of this industry. A fresh study is needed of the numerous little buildings that lie close to Ermine Street in Normangate Field :[21] they can hardly all be workshops. Outside the town to the south-east between Ermine Street and the Nene, is an area of ditched enclosures and disturbed ground that merits investigation. Might this be an 'industrial settlement'? At the other end of the scale are the larger houses in the town, and the well-appointed *villae,* known, for example, at Mill Hill (TL 128972), at Castor village (TL 112984), in Sutton Field (TL 111977), and near Water Newton (TL 112973 and TL 111969).[22] Further work is needed to show whether these are an expression of the prosperity of the industry.

Weston under Penyard might provide an interesting comparison with Chesterton as a small industrial town, but too little is known of it for useful discussion here. The vague discolourations visible from the air indicate ground disturbed by occupation or by iron-working, but there has been no hint so far of substantial buildings, streets or defences. Kenchester,[23] in Herefordshire, closely matches Chesterton, though of less than half the area (17 acres). The irregular hexagonal shape, the stone wall and bastions, the main road with central gutter or drain forming the long axis of the town, the side streets branching off obliquely, and the stone buildings irregularly aligned, are all repeated here, as air photographs show.

Irchester (Northamptonshire),[24] lying in the Nene valley, is another town of much the same size (20 acres). The defences form an irregular pentagon with one very obtuse angle so that the shape approaches a rectangle (Plate V). They comprise a stone wall, eight feet thick, identified by excavation in 1878-9, a broad ditch at least on the west, and, to judge from the way in which the northern half of the town stands high above the fields on either side,[25] a substantial earthen rampart. Within the town occupation-layers may remain to some depth. Photographs taken on a number of occasions show a central north-to-south street from which two side streets branch off in curved lines to east and west. On the west there is a third short straight street. The relation of these streets to the line of the defences invites speculation whether they can possibly be contemporary. The settlement at Irchester evidently developed with irregular streets hardly matching the planned defences that were subsequently provided.

Crop marks reveal a few small, rectangular stone buildings in the southern half of the town, particularly near the central street, while a wide scatter of building debris suggests that there were many more. A square building with a small square foundation set centrally within it looks very like a temple: an octagonal building[26] beside the southernmost street on the west side of the town may well be another. Buildings of some architectural pretensions are suggested by the carved fragments and painted wall plaster recovered in 1878. In spite of damage caused then, by the carting away of masonry, enough buildings and their stratified levels would seem to survive to make a further excavation well worth while.

Of the many settlements that may be presumed along the trunk roads, relatively few, at 'posting-stations' or at river-crossings, grew sufficiently for the question to arise of the provision of defences on any scale. Air photography has thrown new light on a number of these settlements or 'small towns' as they are often dignified, sometimes, indeed, providing the first certain identification of the site, as at Thorpe on Fosse, and at Stretton Bridge on Watling Street. Brough and Thorpe, lying only seven miles apart on the Fosse Way in Nottinghamshire, may be chosen to illustrate the extent of the new information.

Of the Roman settlement at Brough,[27] known by the Latinized name of Crococalana, no surface feature now remains. Knowledge of the place rests upon chance finds of objects and the results of excavation in 1905-6, which together provide evidence of occupation extending over a wide area. Air photography has confirmed this (Plate VII), for crop marks reveal ground so disturbed by large pits, ditches, foundation-trenches, and post-holes, as to give the impression of a long occupation. These disturbances extend over several fields on both sides of the modern road (A46), but have been recorded most clearly on the north-west about the point SK 836585. Moreover, in the field there, lying south-west of Glebe Farm, two broad ditches appear defining the west side, 800 ft long, and parts of the north and south sides of an approximately rectangular enclosure[28] traversed obliquely by the modern road, here not necessarily on the Roman line. The ditches, which are separated by a space over 100 ft wide, seem clearly part of a defensive system, though no trace of a wall or a rampart appears. They cut through the maze of pits and drainage-ditches which extend up to their lips, cover the space between them, and reach far outside. At Brough a straggling settlement that had developed beside the Fosse would seem later in its history to have been provided with defences which included, however, only a small part of the occupied area. The impression conveyed by the heavily disturbed ground, like that obtained by excavation of the settlements at Stretton Mill, or at Mancetter, of closely set timber buildings founded in shallow trenches or post-holes, with numerous pits for storage or refuse: the detailed pattern changing as the same ground was built over more than once. Even if due allowance is made for possible medieval interference, such heavily disturbed ground may well be common in the small road-side settlements of Roman Britain, but a clearer illustration of this than is provided by the photographs of Brough on Fosse taken in 1960 would be difficult to obtain.

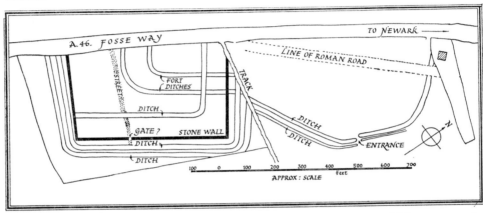

Fig. 1. Sketch plan of Thorpe, Notts., showing the different ditch systems which appear on the aerial photograph.

At Thorpe (Ad Pontem),[29] the sequence of remains is not yet fully determined, but enough is known to show how even these small 'towns' may have an unexpectedly complicated history. At a point (SK 760504) where a meander of the Trent closely approaches the line of the Fosse, air reconnaissance has revealed in arable fields south-east of the modern road (A46) parts of four different enclosures (Plate VI). Two widely spaced ditches are visible for some 300 ft of the south-east side, 100 ft of the south-west side and at the rounded south angle of an enclosure identified by excavation as an early earth-and-timber fort (Fig. 1). Its size is unknown: the Trent would seem to have encroached upon the area to north of the road. Disturbed ground along the Fosse Way indicates civilian settlement, which was enclosed first by a single ditch and later by a broad stone wall and two wide ditches on a parallel alignment further out. The south-east side is about 550 ft in length, measured along the wall: some 350 ft of the north-east side, and rather less of the south-west exist south of the road. At the east and south angles the wall makes an angular change of direction: the broad scatter of light-coloured earth from its weathered debris precludes any useful expression of opinion based on photographs as to whether there were bastions at the angles. A rectangular stone building, at least 90 ft in length, having a single longitudinal division, lies just within the north wall, to which it is parallel, and traces of other stone buildings appear beside the modern road. In the next field to the north, air photographs show part of the outline of an irregular polygonal enclosure, defined by two ditches which embrace an area of some five acres of disturbed ground. A south gate is known at a point where the ditches are staggered. These polygonal ditches and those that go with the stone wall would seem to intersect; photographs do not help here but it may be observed that the stone wall on the north-east side of the rectangular enclosure is continuous, pointing clearly to the conclusion that this work is the later of the two.

The historical significance of these remains will only emerge when further information is available, but it may be observed that the crops growing within the polygonal enclosure disclose a maze of pits and ditches similar to that described at Brough. Whenever, at Thorpe, the need arose for a new defensive system, not only was this planned in depth, involving the construction of a massive stone wall and two widely spaced ditches, but a fresh choice seems to have been made of the precise area to be defended, which lay south-west of that previously enclosed. The sequence here seems closely matched by that at Wall,[30] in Staffordshire, where a first-century fort, or forts, were succeeded by a civilian settlement, and that in turn by a 'town' consisting of a rectangular enclosure of some five acres defended by a stone wall and three ditches, laid out in a new position astride Watling Street.[31] Thorpe provides a striking illustration, likely enough to be repeated elsewhere, that even at the smallest towns the history and structural sequence of the remains is by no means simple.

NOTES

[1] The point is well illustrated by vertical aerial photographs of Cyrene and Leptis Magna in the collection of Hunting Aero-Surveys Ltd., Refs. W.O./2/49/ prints 24795, 24996-7. For recent photographs of certain Roman towns in Italy (Segesta, Falerii Novi, Carsulae, Libarna, and Ferento) see G. Schmiedt, *Contributo della foto-interpretazione . . . in Italia,* Ist. Geog. Militare, Florence, 1964.

[2] *E.g.* Brough, Thorpe, Mancetter, Stretton. The Latinized names are also known of the settlements at, or near, Whilton Lodge, High Cross, Willoughby, and Littleborough, which have so far yielded little to observation from the air though largely free of later buildings. The site at Cave's Inn on Watling Street is too damaged by sand-quarrying for ancient features to be visible.

[3] D. Atkinson: "Report on excavations at Wroxeter 1923-27" (*Birmingham Arch. Soc.,* 1942), for the Forum; J. P. Bushe-Fox: "Excavations on the site of the Roman Town at Wroxeter" (*Soc. of Antiquaries Research Reports,* i (1913), ii (1914), and iv (1916)), for area to south of Forum. For a recent survey of problems at Wroxeter see G. Webster and B. Stanley (*T.Shrop. A.S.,* lvii, pt.2 (1964), 112-131).

[4] A detailed account is in preparation. Neither of the two plans so far published shows all the buildings: *J.R.S.,* xxxix (1949), 105, fig. 22, and *T.Shrop.A.S.,* lvii, pt. 2 (1964), figs. 28-32.

[5] *J.R.S.,* xliii (1953), 84.

6 *J.R.S.*, xlv (1955), 88, pl. xix.

7 *Arch.*, lii (1890) to lxii (1910) *passim*; xcii (1947), 121-167; G. C. Boon, *Roman Silchester* (1957).

8 First recorded by J. Stair about 1744, see Boon, *op. cit.*, 31-32.

9 *Antiquity*, iii (1929), plate facing p. 183.

10 *Antiquity*, xv (1941), pls. i-iii and pp. 120-2.

11 *J.R.S.*, li (1961), 132.

12 *Antiq. J.*, xl (1960), 1-24; xlii (1962), 151, fig. 2, the '1955 ditch'.

13 *Ibid.*, xlii (1962), 153-9, figs. 4-5, pls. xviii-xix.

14 *V.C.H. Oxfordshire*, i (1939), pp. 281-8; *J.R.S.*, xliii (1953), 92.

15 *J.R.S.*, xliii (1953), 90-1, pl. xiii; xlvii (1957), 222-3; xlix (1959), 131; *W.A.M.*, lvi (1957), 241-5; lvii (1960), 233-5, 397.

16 The first of these, a system of two ditches visible on the east, south and west sides of an enclosure having rounded southern angles, and limited to north by low ground next the Kennet, seems to have prompted a symbol for a fort on the Ordnance Survey map of Roman Britain. The position, at the bottom of a narrow valley overlooked from the slope to the south, is a most unmilitary one.

17 *V.C.H. Huntingdonshire*, i (1926), pp. 228-233; Inventory of Hunts. (*R.C.H.M.*, 1926), pp. 52-4; *J.R.S.*, xliii (1953), 91; xlviii (1958), 98.

18 *J.R.S.*, xlviii (1958), 139.

19 E. T. Artis: *The Durobrivae of Antoninus* (1828), pl. xxiii.

20 *J.R.S.*, xlviii (1958), 139-140, fig. 14.

21 Artis, *op. cit.*, pl. xxxix, reproduced in *V.C.H. Hunts.*, i (1926), pl. I no 3, facing p. 230.

22 Artis, *op. cit.*, pl. i.

23 G. H. Jack, "The Romano-British town of Magna, Kenchester" (*Rept. Res. Cmmttee, Woolhope Club* (1916); *J.R.S.*, xliii (1953). 92, pl. xiv, 1; xlviii (1958), 98; *T.Wool.N.F.C.*, xxxv (1956), 138.

24 *V.C.H. Northamptonshire*, i (1902), pp. 178-184, plan fig. 10; *J.R.S.*, liii (1963), 135, fig. 17.

25 It should not be overlooked that this difference in level may in part be due to the effects of ancient ironstone mining.

26 Marked on the plan of 1878-9 (*V.C.H. Northants.*, i, fig. 10) as a circle, but crop marks show clearly an octagonal foundation.

27 *V.C.H. Nottinghamshire*, ii (1910), pp. 11-15; *J.R.S.*, xliii (1953), 91; li (1961), 132, pl. x, 2.

28 The course of the outer ditch on the north side of the enclosure is not clear.

29 *J.R.S.*, xliii (1953), 91; xlviii (1958), 98, pl. xv, 1; li (1961), 177; liv (1964), 159, fig. 12; *T.Thoroton Soc. Nottingham*, xlii (1938), 1-14.

30 *V.C.H.Staffordshire*, i (1908), 193-6; *J.R.S.*, xliii (1953), 83, for the discovery of the triple ditches which are there interpreted as military.

31 *Arch. J.*, cxx (1964), 297-8, fig. 15. The settlement lay mainly on the high ground to north of Watling Street, now occupied by a hamlet. The defended enclosure is dated to the late second century or later.

FORT AND TOWN IN EARLY ROMAN BRITAIN

THE RELATIONSHIP OF CIVIL AND MILITARY SITES IN THE
CONQUEST AND EARLY SETTLEMENT PHASE OF ROMAN BRITAIN

by

Graham Webster

INTRODUCTION

NO EVIDENCE has yet been found in Britain that the native peoples organized themselves in urban communities on the pattern of the Mediterranean world before the Roman conquest. Their settlements in south-east England appear to be no more than a scatter of round huts and enclosures, but by the conquest some communities had at least moved away from the forest retreats and hill-top fortresses to occupy more open ground by rivers, sites more suitable for urban development. Thus in the cases of Camulodunum (Colchester), Verulamium (St Albans), Calleva (Silchester), and Canterbury (Durovernum) there is evidence of pre-Roman occupation and in the first three cases they are sites of mints, the name appearing on the coins. Excavation may reveal further examples of the sites of Romanized towns and settlements developing on pre-Roman sites, especially in south-east England.

Elsewhere the siting of the urban centres appears to originate from military considerations. After the landing in A.D. 43, the decisive Battle of the Medway and the rapid deployment of Roman forces, the greater part of England south of the Humber, Trent, Avon, Severn, and Bristol Channel fell easily, the only exceptions being the two warlike tribes of the south-west, the Durotriges and the tribe known later as the Belgae who gave trouble and may have remained hostile after the swift campaign of 43 under Vespasian, then commander of the second *Augusta*. It can be argued that it was the Roman intention at this stage to convert only this part of the country into a province, i.e. the kingdom of Cunobelinus, the south-western tribes (except the Dumnonii of Devon and Cornwall,) and the two client kingdoms, that of the Iceni and that freshly created for Cogidumnus out of part of the territory of the Atrebates, south of the Thames.

It was the task of Aulus Plautius to establish his forces along the north-western boundary of this area, forming a frontier zone. This arrangement required drastic modification under the second governor Ostorius Scapula who was faced with a serious threat from the tribes of Wales led by the exiled Belgic prince, Caratacus. The central part of the frontier of Plautius was moved forward into the Midlands with a new *limes* eventually established beyond the river Severn. The Claudian attempt to hold only the English lowland and leave the highland zones to the north and west beyond the frontier failed. The tribes on and beyond this frontier, probably inflamed into open hostility by the Druids

31

now established on the Isle of Anglesey, maintained such persistent guerilla activities that Nero was forced into a policy of further conquests. Wales was gradually taken over and further troubles in the north led to advances in this direction later in the first century.

Thus England south of Brigantia (i.e. the Peak and Pennines) was occupied by the Roman Army for only twenty to thirty years and after this developed into the civil part of the province. It can be shown that almost all the towns and small settlements occupied sites adjacent to the earlier forts and must thus have originated as civil settlements outside them, supplying some of the basic needs of troops garrisoned in newly occupied territory. Three of the legionary fortresses, Camulodunum (Colchester), Lindum (Lincoln), and Glevum (Gloucester) became *coloniae,* but a fourth at Viroconium (Wroxeter) developed into the tribal capital of the Cornovii. Sites of auxiliary forts can in some instances be found at varying distances from the later towns, and in others finds of military equipment often indicate the presence of a nearby fort. There are cases, however, beyond the Plautian frontier where the sites of forts are known (as at Greensforge and Metchley) but with no evidence of later civil settlement. In this area, probably more thinly occupied than the south-east, the majority of Britons perhaps moved on elsewhere with the army. It is interesting to observe that inertia on the part of many Britons caused them to remain when the units advanced and they were deprived of the main source of trade. But even after two or three decades it is possible that these sites had become small market centres and they were linked by a road system, now consolidated as part of the Imperial highway system. The needs of the soldiers were to some extent now replaced by travellers using the *mansiones* and *mutationes* set up by the tribes under Imperial direction.

SITES OF FORTS AND TOWNS IN CLOSE PROXIMITY

Legionary fortresses

Camulodunum (Colchester).   Although the actual site of the fortress remains to be found, the evidence of the tombstone of the centurion of the Twentieth, M. Favonius Facilis[1] and the implication of Tacitus[2] are clear evidence of the presence here of Legion XX during the governorship of Aulus Plautius. This is, however, a case of military occupation of the British capital, on a site long established as a native settlement.[3]

Glevum (Gloucester).   There is no direct evidence that this was the site of a legionary fortress, except a lost tombstone of a soldier of Legion XX.[4] The passage of Tacitus, referred to above, the key position of this site commanding the passage of the lower Severn and the items of military equipment have all led to the suggestion that a legion was here, although this has in the past been thought to be the second *Augusta*. The site first considered as that of a legionary fortress was at Kingsholme;[5] no defences or structures have been observed but the quantity of equipment recorded by

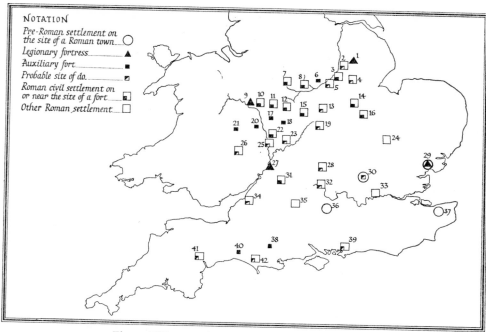

Fig. 2 Military and civil sites in the lowland areas.

1 Lindum (Lincoln)
2 Crococalana (Brough)
3 Ad Pontem (Thorpe-by-Newark)
4 Causennae (Ancaster)
5 Margidunum (Castle Hill)
6 Broxstowe
7 Rocester
8 Derventio (Littlechester)
9 Viroconium (Wroxeter)
10 Uxacona (Red Hill)
11 Pennocrucium
12 Letocetum (Wall)
13 Ratae (Leicester)
14 Great Casterton
15 Manduessedum (Mancetter)
16 Durobrivae (Water Newton)
17 Greensforge
18 Metchley
19 Tripontium (Cave's Inn)
20 Wall Town
21 Bravonium (Leintwardine)

22 Salinae (Droitwich)
23 Alcester
24 Cambridge
25 Worcester
26 Magnis (Kenchester)
27 Glevum (Gloucester)
28 Alauna(?) (Alchester)
29 Camulodunum (Colchester)
30 Verulamium (St. Albans)
31 Corinium (Cirencester)
32 Dorchester-on-Thames
33 Londinium (London)
34 Abonae (Sea Mills)
35 Cunetio (Mildenhall)
36 Calleva (Silchester)
37 Durovernum (Canterbury)
38 Hod Hill
39 Noviomagus (Chichester)
40 Waddon Hill
41 Isca (Exter)
42 Durnovaria (Dorchester)

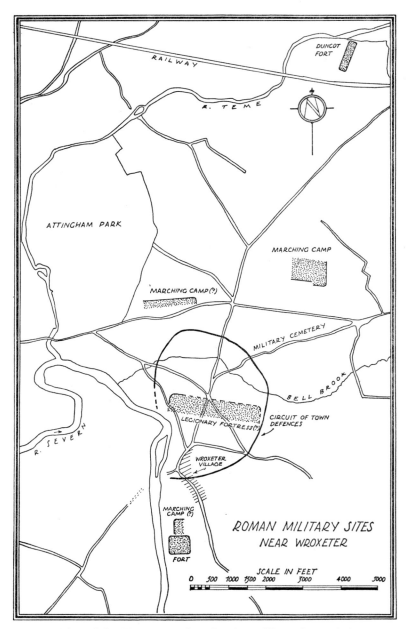

Fig. 3 Plan of the Wroxeter region, showing military sites and the town.

Lysons[6] clearly indicates the presence of an army unit. More recently it has been shown that the *colonia* defences were, in part if not in whole, preceded by military ones as at Lincoln.[7] The change of site may have been due to flooding of the lower one at Kingsholme.

Lindum (Lincoln). This is well-established as the fortress of Legion IX (later replaced by the second Adiutrix) on a 41.5 acre site,[8] which under Domitian became a *colonia*.[9] Although the fine tactical position on the Lincoln Edge, where it is cut by the Witham, would seem to invite earlier defences, there is no positive evidence of any pre-Roman occupation.[10]

Viroconium (Wroxeter). The military situation here on the site of the tribal capital of the Cornovii has become increasingly complicated as new discoveries have been made. The site has long been known as a fortress of Legion XIV from three tombstones.[11] The only archaeological evidence, up to recent times, has been the auxiliary fort, south of the town, found and investigated by Dr J. K. St Joseph[12] and this may account for the tombstone of a trooper of a Thracian cohort.[13] In 1963 Mr Arnold Baker found, from the air, another auxiliary fort on the Tern at Duncot, a mile north of the Roman town and there are traces of at least two marching camps in the vicinity (Fig. 3). The site of the legionary fortress has long been a mystery, but a series of excavations on the site of the Bath-house[14] have shown that the earliest structures consist of three periods of large timber buildings erected in a typically military manner with equipment and pottery datable to *c.* A.D. 60-75. The conclusion that this is part of the legionary fortress is becoming inescapable and may be associated with the defensive ditches first observed by Dr J. K. St Joseph[15] north-west of the Forum, and the early ditches sectioned by Miss Kathleen Kenyon.[16] A section across the street to the north of the town baths also showed a series of timber buildings pre-dating the street system.[17] It would seem therefore that the site of the legionary fortress[18] lies buried deep under the central area of the town and the planning of its remains will always be a difficult problem for any future excavator.[19]

AUXILIARY FORTS ADJACENT TO CIVIL SETTLEMENTS

Ad Pontem (Thorpe-by-Newark). Aerial photographs by Dr J. K. St Joseph reveal a complicated series of defences which have yet to be satisfactorily resolved, one is definitely related to a town wall, but another is considered likely to be military.[20]

Causennae (Ancaster). There is an early ditch system which appears to be on a similar circuit to the later town defences and which three excavators have considered may be of military origin.[21]

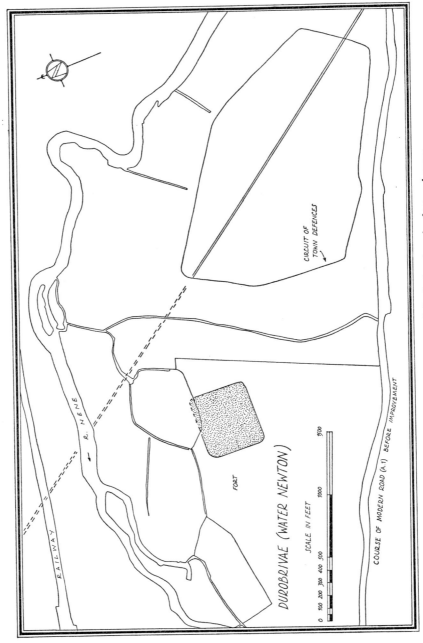

Fig. 4   Plan of Water Newton (*Durobrivae*) showing the fort and town.

Corinium (Cirencester). This important tribal centre has been known to have had military origins since the discovery of the two tombstones[22] of troopers of an *ala Indiana* and an *ala Thracum;* the museum contains a large number of Claudian coins and pieces of military equipment.[23] The northern and eastern defences of one of the forts have now been found in the central area of the town[24] which soon developed over the abandoned military area.

Derventio (Littlechester). Traces of a succession of forts (Flavian to Antonine) have been investigated but the rectangular area of some 9 acres defined by a stone wall now appears to be civil in character.[25]

Dorchester-on-Thames. Much early pottery found during recent excavations[26] at this small Roman town has been tentatively associated with a civil settlement below the later town, but adjacent to a fort, traces of which may have been seen in crop-marks south of the town.

Durobrivae (Water Newton). A small fort between the Roman town and the River Nene has long been known but not yet investigated.[27] (Fig. 4)

Great Casterton. A military site found by Dr J. K. St Joseph and investigated by Professor Sir Ian Richmond[28] exists immediately to the east of the Roman town, the two sets of defences actually overlapping at one point. There were two forts on the same site, the first being the larger. (Fig. 5)

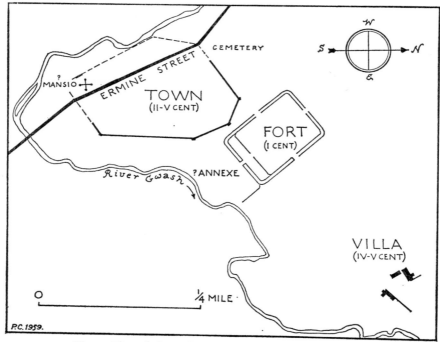

Fig. 5 Plan of Great Casterton, showing fort and town.
(*Published by permission of the University of Nottingham.*)

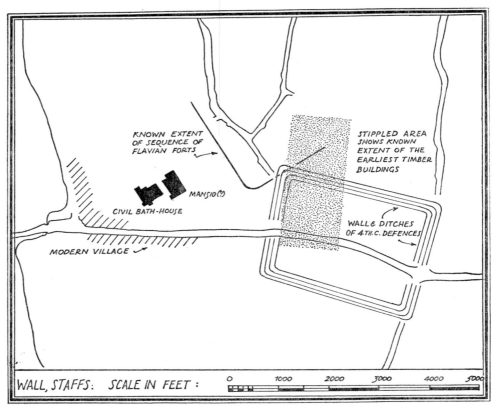

KNOWN EXTENT
OF SEQUENCE OF
FLAVIAN FORTS

STIPPLED AREA
SHOWS KNOWN
EXTENT OF THE
EARLIEST TIMBER
BUILDINGS

MANSIO (?)

CIVIL BATH-HOUSE

WALL & DITCHES
OF 4.TH.C. DEFENCES

MODERN VILLAGE

WALL, STAFFS: SCALE IN FEET :

O   1000   2000   3000   4000   5000

Fig. 6 Plan of Wall, near Lichfield, showing the military sites and the town.

Letocetum (Wall).   The site here is very complicated (Fig. 6). There is a series
of forts beginning with a large Claudian one which may be the fortress of
Legion XIV, prior to its establishment at Wroxeter (see p. 35 above).
Overlying this and occupying the hill-top position are at least three auxiliary
forts with a dating range *c*. A.D. 60-75.[29] To the west down the hill by the
stream is the town Bath-house associated with a building which may be the
mansio.[30] The rest of the town presumably developed along Watling Street
between these buildings and the earlier military ones, but the situation is
further complicated by the presence of a small walled enclosure of fourth-
century date astride the road on the higher ground; but investigations have
so far yielded no trace of buildings of this period within it.[31]

Manduessedum (Mancetter).   The military and civil sites are quite distinct and
separated by the River Anker. The small town lies astride Watling Street
and its defences have been investigated.[32] The military site is half a mile to

the west at the small village of Mancetter. An early ditch has been found[33] and also a hoard of Claudian coins[34] which consists mainly of imitation types which are commonly found on military sites of this period.[35]

Pennocrucium.[36] There are two military sites and a small civil one a little distance from each other (Fig. 7). The auxiliary fort at Stretton Mill, first observed and investigated by Dr J. K. St Joseph,[37] has not produced any closely datable material and a more recent photograph by Mr Arnold Baker clearly shows two forts of different sizes on the same site. About 1,000 yards to the east at Kinvaston there are also forts of two sizes on the same site, the larger being 26 acres.[38] Further excavations have shown that these forts may be Neronian in date[39] and possibly fit into the context of the revolt under Boudicca in A.D. 60.[40] The small civil site bisected by Watling Street has a very similar appearance to the fourth-century enclosure at Letocetum, and a section cut across the defences[41] produced ditch profiles closely resembling those at Wall [42] but with no dating evidence. Letocetum had a substantial wall in addition to the three ditches; there was no evidence of this at Pennocrucium but there is a significant robber trench at the place where a wall might be expected.

Rocester. A small-scale excavation[43] has revealed the presence of a Flavian fort demolished early in the second century and apparently overlain by later civilian occupation with defences enclosing an area of about 9 acres. The two sets of defences may be coincident only in the north-west corner.

Salinae (Droitwich). A fort has been found and partly investigated at Dodderhill[44] on the high ground overlooking the modern town. The period of occupation appears to be from *c.* A.D. 50-70, but a more recent excavation suggests at least two periods with a possible further occupation in the second century;[45] the character of the latter could not however be determined. The civil settlement, based, as the name suggests, on salt extraction, developed on the lower ground. Buildings have been found and excavated in Bays Meadow[46] where there is also the corner of a ditch system, but whether this is part of the town defences is not yet apparent.

Uxacona (Red Hill). This is a site of considerable elevation with good visibility in all directions and at the highest point crop-marks have been recorded of a complicated military site[47] which requires excavation before any assessment of its character can be attempted. Unfortunately the site has been partly obliterated by a large water-tank. A small ditched enclosure lies astride Watling Street but investigations have not so far been rewarding;[48] there seems little doubt however that it was civil in character, bearing a striking resemblance to other sites along Watling Street.

Worcester. The situation here is very obscure but the suggestion of a military site in the area of the Norman Castle, based on the finding of Claudian coins,[49] now seems confirmed by the discovery of a ditch system to the south

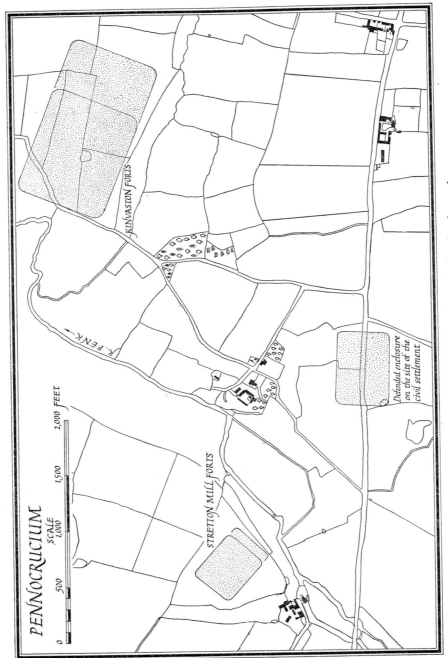

Fig. 7 Plan of Penkridge (*Pennocrucium*), Staffs., showing fort and town.

(Crown Copyright)

of this in an area now occupied by a school swimming bath. These ditches of two periods appear to be military although no conclusive proof was found.[50] Worcester has long been known to have been a Roman town, possibly Vertis,[51] and a late ditch system in Little Fish Street[52] may be part of its defences.

CIVIL SITES WHERE THERE IS EVIDENCE SUGGESTING A MILITARY ORIGIN

Abonae (Sea Mills). The quantity of early coins and pottery[53] and items of equipment[54] clearly indicate the presence of a fort on the Bristol Channel. Little is known, however, of the later town which was probably the ferrying point to Caerwent.

Alcester. The extent of this small town has not yet been defined nor is there any trace of its defences in spite of considerable investigation.[55] One item of horse-gear has been found similar to military examples.[56]

Alchester. A piece of harness of military type has been found in excavations at this small town.[57]

Crococalana (Brough). The site has yielded a decorated cheek-piece of a cavalry parade helmet with a relief of one of the two Dioscuri.[58] The site of the town is known from crop-marks of its defences.[59]

Durnovaria (Dorchester). Claudian coins, and pottery, and items of military equipment[60] strongly suggest a military origin to the town.[61]

Isca (Exeter). Apart from a possible early ditch[62] there is no evidence of a military origin in the form of structures or equipment from this town; but it is included since excavations have produced buildings dated by Claudian pottery.[63] The coin series[64] too is very striking in the predominance of early issues. It seems unlikely that a tribal centre would have developed at such an early date on the extreme frontier during the military occupation which can now be shown to have lasted to c. A.D. 60.[65] No excavations have yet been carried out on the fairly level plateau more than large enough for an auxiliary fort.

Margidunum (Castle Hill). The quantity of early pottery and coins and pieces of military equipment[66] are clear evidence of an early fort. The site of the town is known from the visible earthworks and excavations;[67] it was all thought by the excavator to be part of a Claudian fort.

Magnis (Kenchester). Three undoubted examples of pendants for military horse-trappings have been found during excavations on this small Roman town.[68]

Noviomagus (Chichester). A small collection of military bronzes in the Sadler Collection in the Chichester Museum clearly indicates a military base at an early stage of the conquest.[69] There could have been a landing here with the collaboration of Cogidumnus or a base for the operations of Vespasian in the south-west.[70] In the absence of any pre-Roman occupation and the name given to it, there is a good case for the town having a military origin.[71]

Ratae (Leicester). The presence of Claudian and Belgic pottery is due either to a pre-Roman settlement[72] or to a military origin. The latter seems at present the more likely but equipment is so far limited to a single legionary belt-plate and two other possible items.[73]

Tripontium (Cave's Inn). The precise site of this small civil settlement is not known but it appears to spread along the road from the river Avon in a north-westerly direction for at least half a mile.[74] A military skillet was found in a nearby gravel pit a few years ago,[75] identical with others from undoubted mid-first-century forts.[76]

OTHER TOWNS FOR WHICH CLAIMS COULD OR HAVE BEEN MADE
FOR A MILITARY ORIGIN

Cambridge. A Claudian military site has been claimed on the basis of a ditch below the Shire Hall.[77] It is not however supported by any evidence of equipment and had there been a fort here it is not likely to have been occupied long enough to have been part of the permanent frontier area. There is also the probability of native occupation on the site prior to A.D. 43; a military origin seems therefore unlikely.

Cunetio (Mildenhall). A crop-mark recorded by Dr J. K. St Joseph[78] shows a pair of ditches turning a right-angled corner, the military appearance of which led to their being so designated on the *Ordnance Map of Roman Britain*. Excavations have however shown that this defence system is civil and probably of second-century date.[79]

Londinium (London). The Cripplegate fort has been shown to have probably originated in the early years of the second century[80] reflecting the need for guards and soldiers on special duties concerned with the governor's office and residence. The presence of an earlier fort, or possibly a storage base may be implied in the large quantity of equipment,[81] and leather work[82] found in the Walbrook. The crossing of the Thames, so vital for communications and the potential harbour facilities, would also certainly have made London an important trading centre, perhaps even prior to A.D. 43, so the theory of military origin cannot have the weight of these others factors.

NOTES

[1] *Roman Colchester,* pl. i(a) and pp. xxv and xxvi; *V.C.H. Roman Essex* (1963), 2-5.

[2] Tacitus, *Annals,* xii, 32, Ostorius Scapula founded a *colonia* here in order to release a legion for his campaign against Caratacus.

[3] *Camulodunum.*

[4] *C.I.L.,* vii, 1339. There is also the tombstone of Rufus Sita, a trooper of the Sixth Cohort of Thracians, found in the same cemetery area.

[5] By Mr Charles Green, *J.R.S.,* xxxii (1942), 39.

[6] *Reliquae Britannico Romanae,* ii, pls. xi-xv.

[7] By Mrs H. O'Neil, *T.B.G.A.S.,* lxxxi (1962), 10-40, where there is also a reassessment of the military situation by Professor Sir Ian Richmond.

[8] A series of investigations of the military defences culminated in an excavation by Mr D. F. Petch in which he demonstrated the coincidence of *colonia* with legionary defences on the southern side, *Arch. J.,* cxvii for 1960 (1962), 40-70.

[9] *Arch. J.,* ciii for 1946 (1947), 29.

[10] The evidence of post-holes pre-dating the Roman defences advanced by the author in 1949 (*J.R.S.,* xxxix (1949), 60-62) must now be suspect, since with further experience in this type of limestone he would now prefer a natural explanation.

[11] *C.I.L.,* vii, 154, 155, and 157; these have been fully published by Haverfield, *V.C.H. Shrops.,* i (1908), 244-6, the only additional knowledge is that No. 157 has now been refound and is in the Rowley House Museum, Shrewsbury, the traces of the numbers on the last surviving line can be interpreted as ...XI]II ..., which makes it very probably a soldier of the XIV. In the two complete examples, the titles MARTIA VICTRIX awarded to the legion after its share in the defeat of Boudicca in A.D. 60 do not appear, and this would seem to place them prior to this date. The appearance of a memorial of a soldier of *Legio XX, C.I.L.,* vii, 156, led to a suggestion by Haverfield that this legion too may have been stationed at Wroxeter. This point was taken up more strongly by Collingwood, *Roman Britain and the English Settlements* (1937), p. 93, and the idea of a double legionary fortress came into being. The stone, however. is that of a *beneficiarius legati provinciae,* i.e. an orderly on the staff of the governor of Britain, and who on detached duty might have died and been buried anywhere.

[12] *T.B.A.S.,* lxix for 1951 (1952), 54 and fig. 2.

[13] *C.I.L.,* vii, 158.

[14] Organized as training schools in excavation techniques by the Extra-Mural Department of the University of Birmingham.

[15] *J.R.S.,* xlv (1955), 88 and pl. xix.

[16] *Arch.,* lxxxviii (1940), pl. xx, Sections A, B, and C; the characteristic turf rampart and rectangular slot at the bottom of one of the ditches is significant, as is also the lack of alignment with the later town defences.

[17] Report forthcoming.

[18] The alterations which have been noted can be associated no doubt with legionary movements, the Twentieth probably replacing the Fourteenth after A.D. 69 when the latter was withdrawn from Britain.

[19] These began 8 ft. below the present ground level on the Baths site.

[20] *J.R.S.,* liv (1964), 159 and fig. 12.

[21] This was first observed by Mr Charles Green in the south-west corner (*J.R.S.,* xlvii (1957), 210), later Mrs H. O'Neil recorded a ditch on the west side and more recently Mr M. W. Barley on the east. If this is a single system it would be a fort unusual not only in size (9 acres), but also in that it coincided with later civic defences. It would be wise to suspend assessment until more evidence comes to light. There are no military objects recorded, but the early coins are significant (*Arch. J.,* ciii for 1946 (1947), 19).

[22] *C.I.L.,* vii, 66 and 68; *Arch.,* lxix for 1917-18 (1920), 185-7.

[23] *Arch. J.,* cxv for 1953 (1960), 73-75

[24] By Mr J. S. Wacher, *Antiq. J.,* xlii (1962), 3-5; xliii (1963), 15-16; xlv (1965), 97-101.

[25] *D.A.J.,* lxxxi (1961), 85-110. The military and civil sites although occupying the same site at the point investigated, are on different alignments.

26 By Professor Sheppard Frere, *Arch. J.*. cxix for 1962 (1964), 128-9.

27 *Antiquity*, xiii (1939), 178 and 455; *J.R.S.*, xxix (1939), 208; xliii (1953), pl. ix, No. 1.

28 *Great Casterton*, III, 13-17 and report forthcoming.

29 *T.B.A.S.*, lxxix for 1960 and 1961 (1964), 11-23.

30 *T.B.A.S.*, lxxiv for 1956 (1958), 12-29.

31 *Lichfield and S. Staffs.A. & Hist.S.*, v (1964), 1-50.

32 By Mr Adrian Oswald, *T.B.A.S.*, lxxiv for 1956 (1958), 30-52.

33 *Ibid.*, 36.

34 *T.B.A.S.*, lxxix for 1960 and 1961 (1964), 117-120.

35 C. H. V. Sutherland. *Romano-British Imitations of Bronze Coins of Claudius I*, (1935).

36 "The site is a mile west of the Gailey cross-roads and its name is usually associated with the modern village of Penkridge, the name of which according to Ekwall (*Dictionary of English Place-Names*, 1960) is derived from Pennocrucium. The meaning of the latter appears to be 'the mound on a hill'. The difficulties here are that the Roman site is not on a hill but on a very slight plateau by the River Penk, also that Penkridge is three miles to the north-east. The name may originally have been derived from a native hill-fort on the higher ground to the south-west since it does not seem to apply to either the Roman civil or military sites, none of which are on high ground. The name of the modern settlement, Penkridge, seems more likely to have come from the river name, now the Penk, but in the tenth century the Penchrich and which in turn may have originated from the Celtic name for the Roman settlement."

37 *T.B.A.S.*, lxix for 1951 (1953), 50-52.

38 Also discovered and first investigated by Dr J. K. St Joseph, *Ibid.*, 52-54; *J.R.S.*, xlviii (1958), 94-95.

39 *T.B.A.S.*, lxxiii for 1955 (1957), 100-108.

40 D. R. Dudley and Graham Webster, *The Rebellion of Boudicca* (1960), 109.

41 *T.B.A.S.*, lxxiv for 1956 (1958), 1-5 and fig. 3.

42 *T.B.A.S.*, lxxv for 1957 (1959), fig. 2 on p. 25.

43 *N. Staffs J. of F.S.*, ii (1962), 37-52.

44 By Dr J. K. St Joseph, *T.B.A.S.*, lxii for 1938 (1943), 27-31.

45 By Mr D. B. Whitehouse, but only a very small area was explored, *T.W.A.S.*, xxxix for 1962 (1963), 55-58.

46 *T.B.A.S.*, lxiv for 1941 and 1942 (1946), 39-52; lxxv for 1957 (1959), 1-23.

47 First observed by Dr J. K. St Joseph, *J.R.S.*, xliii (1953), 84; a photograph by Mr Arnold Baker appears in *T.Shrop.A.S.*, lvii (1964), pl. xxii.

48 By the Wrekin Archaeological Group, the site available was limited and there had been much modern disturbance, *Shropshire News Letter*, No. 13 (1960), 4.

49 *V.C.H.Worcs.*, i, 205 and fig. 3.

50 Work carried out by the Severn Valley Research Group, report forthcoming.

51 Following the suggested grouping of the lists in the Ravenna Cosmography by Professor Sir Ian Richmond, *Arch.*, xciii (1949), Map iii; *T.W.A.S.*, xxxvii for 1960 (1961), 43-44.

52 *T.W.A.S.*, xxxv for 1958 (1959), 67-70.

53 *T.B.G.A.S.*, lxi (1939), 202; lxv (1944), 195; lxvi (1945), 294; lxviii (1949), 184; lxxi (1954), 70.

54 Listed in *Arch. J.*, cxv for 1958 (1960), 89.

55 By groups from the Birmingham Archaeological Society and the University of Birmingham Arch. Soc.; *T.B.A.S.*. lxxvi for 1958 (1960), 10-18 and reports forthcoming and in 1965 a large-scale emergency excavation directed by Miss C. Mahany.

56 *T.B.A.S.*, lxvi for 1945 and 1946 (1950), pl. xii, fig. 1, No. 53.

57 *Antiq. J.*, xii (1932), pl. xviii, No. 8.

58 *Arch.*, lviii (1893), 573 and pl. lv; the piece is now in Newark Museum.

59 *J.R.S.*, xliii (1953), 91.

60 Listed in *Arch. J.*, cxv for 1958 (1960), 79.

61 Apart from the excavations on a town house at Colliton Park (Interim reports in *P.D.N.H.S.*, lix (1938), 1-14; lx (1939), 51-65), and an investigation of the defences (*ibid.*, lxxv (1955), 72-83), little work has been done on the town.

[62] This was found in excavations near the south gate in 1964 and ran at right-angles to the line of the civil defences. It produced pre-Flavian pottery from the primary silt and may have been associated with military enclosures near the river rather than part of an actual fort—(information kindly supplied by Lady Fox).

[63] A. Fox, *Roman Exeter* (1952).

[64] *Ibid.*, fig. 7.

[65] *P.D.N.H.S.*, lxxxii (1961), 91-92; lxxxvi (1965), 135-149.

[66] From the various excavations of Dr Felix Oswald, possibly on the site of a fort annexe.

[67] *J.R.S.*, xxxi (1941), fig. 4.

[68] Listed in *Arch. J.*, cxv for 1958 (1960), 83. The town itself is well defined and was first investigated by G. H. Jack, *Excavations on the Site of the Romano-British Town of Magna, Kenchester, Herefordshire*, during the years 1912-13, 1916, and 1924-25, 1926, published as Research Reports of the Woolhope Club; since then detailed investigations have been carried out on the town defences, *T.Wool.N.F.C.*, xxxv (1957), 138-145; xxxvi (1959), 100-116; xxxvii (1963), 149-178.

[69] Graham Webster and D. R. Dudley, *The Roman Conquest of Britain*, 1965, Appendix v.

[70] This is hardly the place to enter into the difficulties raised by the historical account of Dio and the Temple inscription recording the honours given to Cogidumnus. Intriguing possibilities have been suggested by Professor C. F. C. Hawkes (*Bagendon*, 56-67); see also fn. 69, p. 58-60. Timber granaries of Claudian date found by Mr Barry Cunliffe below the villa at Fishbourne (*Antiq. J.*, xliii (1963), 34-35; xlv (1965), 2-3), may have belonged to a large store base at Bosham Harbour and if so attested this could well have been one of Vespasian's bases for his rapid western advance of A.D. 43.

[71] The finds from Selsey strongly suggest that an important native site existed here, but has since been eroded by the sea.

[72] A suggestion by Miss K. M. Kenyon, *Jewry Wall*, 9.

[73] *Arch. J.*, cxv for 1958 (1960), 84; the stamped tile should be discounted since there is no evidence of any military tiles in Britain bearing stamps before the end of the first or beginning of the second century.

[74] Work by the Rugby Archaeological Society in advance of gravel workings, interim note in *T.B.A.S.*, lxxx for 1962 (1965), 80-82.

[75] Now in Warwick Museum, it is stamped with the maker's name MATVRVS. F on the handle, note forthcoming; also *J.R.S.*, li (1961), 195.

[76] Broxtowe, *Antiq. J.*, xix (1939), pl. lxxxvii, and Gloucester, *Arch. J.*, cxv for 1958 (1960), pl. ix(b) (in the British Museum).

[77] *R.C.H.M.*, *City of Cambridge*, i (1949), xxxvi and 7-8.

[78] *J.R.S.*, xliii (1953), 90-91.

[79] Information kindly supplied by Mr K. Annable who directed the work, *W.A.M.*, xlvi (1956), 241-45; *J.R.S.*, xlix (1959), 131.

[80] *J.R.S.*, xl (1950), 107-109; xli (1951), 134; xlii (1952), 97; xlvii (1957), 219-220; xlix (1959). 125-126; l (1960), 229.

[81] *Small Finds from the Walbrook 1955-59*, and list in *Arch. J.*, cxv for 1958 (1959), 84-86.

[82] There are interesting collections of leather work in the British Museum and Guildhall Museum which would well repay close study.

ROMAN EXETER (*Isca Dumnoniorum*)

ORIGINS AND EARLY DEVELOPMENT

by

Aileen Fox

Isca, the cantonal centre for the *civitas* of the Dumnonii, is a town founded in the early fifties. It is sited on the river Exe after which it was named *Isca*, meaning, according to Sir Ifor Williams, 'river full of fish', a pleasant ancient tribute to a present-day delicacy, Exe salmon. It was sited at the first convenient crossing of the navigable river, near the head of former tidal water and thus, accessible by land and sea, was well fitted as a centre for trade and travellers: to this it owed its prosperity in Roman and historic times.

The actual position was on the end of a spur sloping down at right angles to the river with a steep scarp to the Longbrook valley on its northern side; this offers a ready-made outline for a hill-fort, but there is no evidence it was so fortified in the Iron Age. A recent exposure of the city rampart in West Street above the river showed that, as elsewhere, this was a unitary Roman work. The references to an ancient British fortress in Exeter called Caer Wysc, which give rise to misconception in some popular works, are derived from Geoffrey of Monmouth and like much of what he wrote is a plausible invention. Nevertheless it is probable, though not yet proved stratigraphically, that there was some sort of Iron age trading post on the hillside. Three copper coins of Greek cities in South Italy, Paestum and Velia, dating from the third and second centuries B.C. were found unstratified in excavations in Smythen Street in 1931[1] and a fragment of a painted Gaulish bowl dating from the second half of the first century B.C. turned up in 1946, in the gravel laid for the Forum *c.* A.D. 80;[2] all these are highly suggestive of the activities of merchant-traders from overseas over an extended period. It remains uncertain whether there was still a nucleus of Iron Age population on the site in 1 A.D. A native element is always apparent in the coarse pottery from the earliest Roman layers, principally the ribbed bead-rim bowls and jars with counter-sunk lug handles, which are characteristic of the late Iron Age in E. Devon and Dorset (Southern Third C.),[3] but as yet no pits or other signs of pre-Roman occupation have been found. There was, however, a large Iron Age population in the surrounding countryside, living in a variety of hill-forts mostly of modest scale,[4] and from the Roman point of view the source from which the first decurions could be enrolled and drawn into administration and town life.

The founding of the town goes back to late Claudian times, in my view to the governorship of Ostorius Scapula, in whose time Tacitus tells us "the nearest parts of Britain were gradually shaped into a province." The Roman forces first reached the south-west at the end of the hard-fought campaign against the Durotriges, in which Vespasian in command of the Second Augustan Legion had taken more than twenty hill-forts, including, of course, Maiden Castle. There is no evidence to suggest that the Dumnonii offered much resistance: indeed west of the Exe most of their *oppida* were designed more for the needs of stock-keeping than for tribal defence, with small-scale ramparts and loose-knit plan, often with incomplete perimeter, and could not have long withstood a Roman assault.[5] At any rate there is no sign of a fort having been planted in the Exe valley at this time[6] and no finds of military equipment have been recorded from the city or its environs. This is in contrast to the Durotriges who were placed under close military supervision as the excavations at Hod Hill and Waddon Hill have so clearly demonstrated. The southern end of the Fosse Way would at this period have been a dividing line between the friendly Dumnonian territory on the west and that of the Durotrigian foes recently overcome on the east, which had to be held down.

Another indication that the Dumnonii were allied comes from the discovery that the two signal stations on the North Devon coast belong to this early conquest period and not to the fourth century as so long supposed. Excavations in 1963 by Dr W. Ravenhill and myself at Old Burrow, Countisbury, showed that it was occupied temporarily in Claudian times, whilst Martinhoe, excavated in 1960-61, was a semi-permanent post occupied throughout the reign of Nero.[7] Their function was to keep watch in conjunction with the fleet based at Abonae (Sea Mills) on the troublesome Silures in South Wales. Their small garrisons could hardly have been planted in isolation on the Exmoor coast with hill-forts in their immediate neighbourhood without some general agreement with the tribes. Similarly the fact that the Romans were so quickly able to locate and work the silver-lead mines on Mendip by A.D. 49 is best understood when it is realized that these were situated in friendly Dumnonian territory. This is clear from the distribution of decorated Third B pottery[8] which extends eastwards from the peninsula to the crest of the Mendips where the mines are situated. It is also apparent that the inhabitants of Meare and Glastonbury lake-villages had used the lead for manufacture previously.

I have dwelt in some detail on the Iron Age and historical background because Dr Graham Webster has expressed doubts whether the early occupation at Exeter is really a civil settlement. He has argued very plausibly that there ought to be a Roman fort here as a terminus of the Claudian campaign to control the river crossing and the traffic on the estuary.[9] So, with this in mind, let us look again at what we actually know from excavations, which were mostly carried out under the handicaps of the immediate post-war epoch.

The main feature was the location in South Street in 1946[10] of what must have been the main road to the river crossing, since it was aligned on the later Roman West gate, with timber buildings fronting on it on either side. Though well metalled it was only 10 ft wide with a central drain, into which refuse had been thrown. The buildings were constructed with a framework of close-set

Fig. 8. Plan of Roman Exeter.

driven posts with an infilling of bedded wattling. Inevitably, as in any city excavation, their remains were incomplete but there was enough to indicate a plan and to establish their civilian character. One had a principal room 37 by 25 ft, flanked by a passage or verandah at the rear, and with an extension, perhaps a lean-to, at the side. In the centre of the floor, which was of clean clay and had been sanded, there was an open tile hearth. In the extension, bronze and enamel working in crucibles of Iron Age type had been carried on under squalid conditions, for the floor was deep in dirt, soot, and charcoal, with much food refuse and broken pottery. Such findings are not compatible with a first-century military occupation where discipline would ensure that barracks were kept clean, rubbish removed, and that fire-risks were eliminated by cooking in field ovens away from timber buildings. On the other hand we can see, at Verulamium, the same features in the early timber buildings excavated by Professor Frere on the Watling Street, with their frontage close to the road, an open tile hearth in one of them, and remains of small-scale industry.[11]

The South Street buildings were occupied for about 20 years from A.D. 50/55-75, before they were dismantled to make way for an extensive open gravel courtyard, probably the Forum. In Bartholomew Street East, however, excavated in 1959 the timber buildings were of rather later date.[12] (Fig. 9) The first signs of occupation here were a number of scattered ovens and smelting places together with iron slag, pieces of crucibles, and tuyères; coins of Claudius and Nero were associated. This was succeeded c. A.D. 65-70 by a row of small buildings lined up on a substantial metalled east to west road, more than 14 ft wide, with a camber and side-drain. Their construction was similar to those in South Street with a frame of close-set driven posts and infilling of wattle and daub. Again their complete plan was unobtainable because of disturbance, but there was nothing reminiscent of a barrack block. One apparently consisted of a large front room, perhaps a shop, with a smaller inner one flanked by passages and an open space at the rear. They had been destroyed by fire c. A.D. 80-85, which burnt the daub walls to a brick-like consistency or caused them to collapse as a heap of clay. Though the road was repaired twice subsequently, the site, which lies close to the city northern defences, was not built on again in Roman times.

This completes the evidence for the first phase at Isca: all structures found are consistent with a civil settlement and no objects have been found in them to suggest the presence of soldiers.[13] Thereafter the township prospered, unaffected by the troubles of A.D. 60-61, as shown by the occurrence of imported luxuries like decorated Samian and glass[14] and by coins series[15] assiduously recorded by a local antiquary Captain T. P. Shortt in the early nineteenth century, which indicates that much money was circulating in the town in pre-Flavian and early Flavian times: in this respect it compares with what we know at Verulamium.

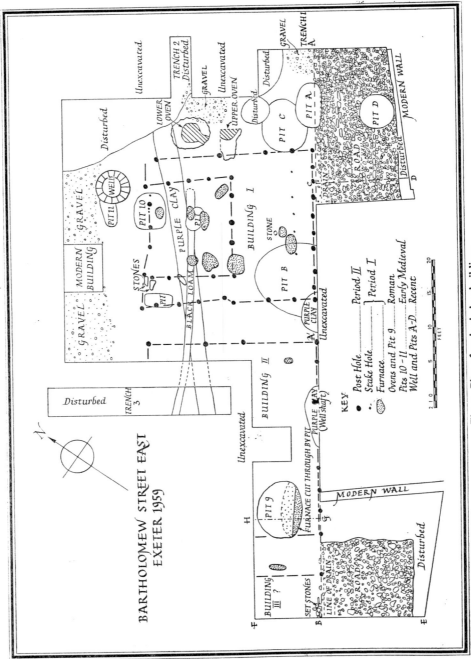

Fig. 9. Plan of early timber buildings.

Public buildings in stone were begun in the centre of Isca *c.* A.D. 80-85; in this we can recognize the effects of Agricola's liberal policy. Very little remains, just enough to identify in 1946 an open court and ambulatory situated to the west of South Street, and held to belong to the Forum, and a plunge bath and stone-arched waste conduit belonging to the Public Baths in the Deanery grounds opposite. As at Caerwent, these two municipal buildings must have been close together.

The extent of the Baths is now better known (Fig. 8): a north-south road found in the Bear Street excavations in 1953[16] indicated its eastern limits, whilst the remaking of South Street in 1955 revealed massive concrete foundations beneath the highway, some of walls, others of substructures to counteract the slope. Similar discoveries were recorded by Captain Shortt in 1830-40. We now know that the Baths covered an area of over 20,000 square feet.

The Roman street grid is now beginning to appear though no insula can yet be defined (Fig. 8). It is apparent that the medieval street system, now so rapidly disappearing, only occasionally embodies a survival from Roman times.[17]

NOTES

[1] Montgomery Neilson, *P.Dev.A.E.S.,* i (1931), 128, 141 and pl. C.
[2] A. Fox, *Roman Exeter,* 76 and pl. X, D.
[3] *Ibid.,* figs. 14-16; and J. Brailsford, *P.P.S.,* xxiv (1958), 101.
[4] *Ibid.,* fig. 2.
[5] A. Fox, "South-western hill-forts" in (ed.) S. S. Frere *Problems of the Iron Age,* 35.
[6] But see note 9.
[7] *J.R.S.,* lii (1962), 184, fig. 28.
[8] South-western hill-forts, *loc. cit.,* 52, fig. 20.
[9] The discovery in August 1964 of a deep well-cut ditch at the South Gate suggests that such a military post existed 300 yards south of the civil settlement and separated from it by the Combe Street valley. The ditch was over 8 ft wide and 5 ft deep, running at right angles to and beneath the later City Wall. A Samian base and a bead-rim bowl from the silt indicate its early Roman origin. This was confirmed in 1965 in a second section by finding a Claudian type amphora neck with peaked handles, at the bottom of the ditch. The situation was well chosen for a small fort, on level ground above the steep rise from an obvious landing-place on the Exe at the Customs House, and defended on the north and south by the Combe Street and Shutebrook valleys: see *Roman Exeter,* fig. 1.
[10] *Roman Exeter,* 7 and 30 ff.
[11] *Antiq. J.,* xxxix (1959), 5, fig. 2.
[12] Not yet published; note in *J.R.S.,* (1960), 231.
[13] See note 9.
[14] *P.Dev.A.E.S.,* iv (1951), 106.
[15] *Roman Exeter,* 61, fig. 7.
[16] *P.Dev.A.E.S.,* v (1953), 30.
[17] An internal gate tower of the South Gate discovered in 1964 confirms that the Roman gates were in approximately the same positions as their medieval successors.

DATING TOWN BUILDINGS AND STRUCTURES
by
B. R. Hartley

THE need for sound dating-evidence for our structural remains in the towns of Roman Britain is obvious. Any individual site may produce series of structures capable of being related to each other and so arranged in chronological sequence, but unless they can be dated absolutely and considered alongside other parts of the same site or comparable development in other towns the stuff of history will not be there. A firm chronology does not give automatic insight into all aspects of Romano-British towns, but without one we should simply have a chaos of disjointed fragments of information—a state of affairs not unknown for some provinces of the Roman Empire. Any appreciation of the present situation must take into account two main aspects of the subject: first, the nature and quality of the evidence available; secondly, its application to the structures.

In discussing sources of dating-evidence pride of place must necessarily be given to contemporary or near-contemporary historical accounts, partly because all our other sources of evidence rest ultimately upon them, partly because, although the record for Britain is undeniably meagre, not least for the Cantonal capitals, such information as we have is fundamentally important and takes us, at the best, behind the structures to the institutions underlying them and hence to the salutary reminder that we are, or should be, dealing ultimately with people and ideas, not just things. For instance, if we had no Tacitus or Dio, how would we treat the establishment of the *colonia* at Colchester or arrive at a date for, or understanding of, the Boudiccan rebellion and all that lay behind these events? Without Suetonius would we ever stop to consider the possibility that busts of Titus with honorific inscriptions adorned our towns in the first century?[1] Of course, most of the facts recorded for towns in Britain are commonplaces that we tend to accept automatically. We should tend to look, in the light of Spartianus' oblique reference[2] and our general knowledge of Hadrian, for signs of his influence in our towns, for instance. But there are other sources that we have not yet exploited fully: one, curiously neglected and yet surely worth consideration, is what Ammianus Marcellinus recounts of the aftermath of the *barbarica conspiratio* of A.D. 367. Theodosius is explicitly said to have restored the *civitates*,[3] at this period surely a reference to the towns rather than tribal units. We surely need to ask whether the observed fourth-century modernization of town defences by adding projecting artillery platforms was part of the Theodosian programme. Our archaeological evidence for one of the structures gives a *terminus post quem* of A.D. 354, which is suspiciously close to

Theodosius.[4] And the use of these structures points to a period of general reorganization, since whatever 'militia' there may have been manning town defences in earlier days, the bastions imply the use of essentially professional weapons calling for a high degree of technical competence both in use and in maintenance, whether *ballistae* or *onagri* were in question. On this matter Ammianus is clearly not conclusive, but nevertheless the question needs putting.

In contrast with many other provinces, inscriptions are notoriously lacking from our towns. It is almost unbelievable that so few public buildings and not a single town wall in Britain can be dated epigraphically, but such material as we have is vital. At Verulamium the Forum, if dated on purely archaeological evidence and with Tacitus in mind[5] might well be assigned to Agricola. With its inscription,[6] we can see at once that though Agricola completed the structure, it must have been Frontinus, or even Cerialis, who initiated the building.[7] Both the Verulamium and Wroxeter[8] *fora* are dated to a year; less precise, but perhaps even more important, because so unexpected, is the theatre inscription from Brough-Petuaria, attesting administrative institutions as well as the structure.[9] Similarly, the famous Cogidubnus inscription from Chichester or its vicinity[10] and the less well-known pedestal from Caerwent[11] are vital to our story. Structures are implicit in both, but the attestation of the *collegia* with all that they mean for town-life is more important.

Coins as a source of dating-evidence are often given rank immediately after the historians and inscriptions.[12] At best this may be true, but there are abundant pitfalls to avoid. There is above all the notoriously difficult task of estimating the length of circulation of a coin before its loss. Wear is not always readily to be distinguished from corrosion in the ground, and inevitably single coins bring uncertainty, since they may have come back into circulation, sometimes in mint condition, after inactivity in a savings hoard. Then, too, estimates of wear are necessarily subjective, and can only be taken as giving a general indication of the likely minimum life of a coin before loss. Nevertheless, this does not absolve us from recording states of wear in coin lists in excavation reports, and a plea to both archaeologists and numismatists is perhaps needed here.[13]

For the earlier Roman period in Britain coins are relatively uncommon as site-finds compared with other kinds of dating-evidence and on the whole their greatest use for dating falls in the later third and fourth centuries.[14] Nonetheless, a coin beneath a structure, always assuming that intrusion can be ruled out,[15] has the merit of giving a firm *terminus post quem*, and that is not to be despised.

Most of our dating rests unavoidably on what may be termed second-class material such as pottery. On the whole imported wares are most useful for the first and second centuries, British products later. Among the imports samian ware stands out, alike in the quantity in which it occurs, the precision with which it may be dated, and the attention with which it has been studied. Like all pottery, it tended to have a relatively short life and in towns, as opposed to military sites, we almost certainly do not have to reckon with lengthy storage in shops before sale. In general the manufacture of decorated samian bowls of the first or the early second century may be dated to within fifteen or twenty years.[16] For the later second century the situation is not so happy, and much of the dating done before the 1950s is in need of revision. The publication of Stanfield and Simpson's *Central Gaulish Potters* has been a useful corrective, though here and there the pendulum may perhaps have swung a trifle too far, but a glance at the chronological table in that work shows how much is still to be done in defining more closely the periods of potters' activities. Further advance must rest primarily on the results from dated military sites with divided Antonine occupations[17] or occupations restricted to part of the period,[18] but a revival of interest in the Gaulish manufactories is now beginning to help by providing large groups of contemporary material for study. Plain samian is naturally less helpful, and many forms which changed relatively little over decades will never be closely datable. Perhaps the most fruitful source for the future will lie in potters' stamps on samian. The late Dr Felix Oswald's pioneer work is now outdated and a thorough reappraisal, based on study of the individual dies, is now in progress and already begins to show promise.[19]

Other imported wares bulk less large in the record and can rarely be dated with the same precision as samian ware, though stamped *amphorae* can be particularly helpful.[20] St Rémy ware is imperfectly known, and while much of the lead-glazed pottery in Britain assigned to that centre is pre-Flavian, it is now thought that St Rémy produced similar ware at a much later date,[21] and the possibility of some later export to Britain cannot be excluded. Then, too, lead-glazed vessels seem to have been made in this island.[22] Rhenish ware, a form of colour-coated ware with black glossy surface, is one of the latest imports to reach Britain in quantity. Again, however, much is to be learned before a reliable chronology is available, and the realization that some of the ware normally termed 'Rhenish' was made at Lezoux complicates the issue. On northern military sites such ware is apparently current only at the very end of the second century, and in the first half of the third century,[23] but it does not follow that this applies in southern towns. Nor is it always easy to distinguish British imitations from the originals.

When we turn to British products it is primarily the pottery that achieved wide distribution which helps most. Mortaria and colour-coated wares appear both on military sites and in towns, and the same kilns often served both markets. Mortaria, because often stamped with potters' names or marks from the Flavian period to the late second century, are easily traced and this helps dating on the one hand and assessment of the growth and fluctuations in the pottery industry and its marketing-patterns on the other. The colour-coated ware made in the Nene Valley[24] or at Colchester[25] cannot be used so precisely as mortaria, since it is not always possible to be sure of its origin, but it is one of the chief means of dating late Roman deposits. Recent results from the Nene Valley suggest a slightly earlier date of introduction than has usually been postulated;[26] and the excavations there, so far unpublished in detail, should help to allow more precise dating for the third- and fourth-century types. Even so, the close dating possible for some samian ware is unlikely to be emulated.

In other classes of coarse pottery there is obviously a great range of dating-values, and it is impossible to deal adequately with the subject here. Mr J. P. Gillam's study of coarse pottery from northern sites is invaluable for that region[27] and important for others, for his evidence for types supplied from midland and southern kilns is relevant to many of our towns. But a word of caution may be needed: it is essential that identity of form and fabric should be established before the northern dating is applied elsewhere. Furthermore, it seems likely that some types were distributed locally from kilns in the lowlands before they became established in the northern markets. Much of the pottery found in the British towns is from local kilns, sometimes built, it would seem, to supply only the nearest town. This can normally only be dated very loosely on general typological grounds or at sites where abundant groups of the pottery are associated with coins or other pottery in the categories already discussed. At this level we are two stages removed from the basic dating provided by history and inscriptions.[28]

Now we must consider the application of the available dating-evidence in practice. Historical sources and inscriptions will not be discussed further, since the problems involved are peculiar to the individual instance and are usually self-evident. Most of what has been said so far on pottery concerns dating of manufacture, but the excavator is concerned with material that has been used and discarded. Survival of a pot in use for an abnormally long period is a hazard that may be difficult to estimate; such points as the degree of wear on the foot-ring of a samian vessel or the thickness of fur in cooking pots in regions with hard water may give useful hints. In general, however, instances of long life will not be a serious problem, since large groups of material are normally in question and survivals will stand out. More serious, particularly in towns, can be the proportion of residual or rubbish-survival pottery in a given deposit. The cutting of ditches, of deep foundation trenches for public buildings and of pits frequently turns up much earlier material into later layers.[29] Extremely careful assessment of particular groups is called for, and often it may be a matter of picking out a handful of sherds truly contemporary with the deposition of a layer from a large group. This applies with particular force to ramparts, for the pottery in the body of an earthwork is almost inevitably entirely residual. That such material can only give a *terminus post quem* dating is obvious, but this simple fact cannot be overstressed.

In dealing with buildings, material sealed by wall or floor may be used with confidence to give a firm *terminus post quem,* but material overlying a floor is a very different matter. In general it will only have got there after that floor ceased to be used. Mosaics depicting unswept floors may have been fashionable gimmicks of the Graeco-Roman world,[30] but this does not justify the belief that Romano-British householders tolerated broken sherds or bones on their living-room floors any more than we should. Apart from destruction deposits, material lying on or over floors should be treated with great caution. It is quite possible for it to be partly or largely earlier than the building itself.

Pits are often important in towns as on other sites. Two hazards need emphasizing. First, that consolidation of the original filling usually means development of a hollow which will sooner or later be filled with fresh material. Secondly, that in a hard subsoil the soft fillings of pits often attract burrowing animals which leave temporary or permanent voids down which later material may penetrate in earlier filling. Very careful observation may be needed to detect and allow for this possibility.

It may now be helpful to turn to some of the specific problems of dating raised by Romano-British towns. One of the most revealing pieces of information we can have about any town is its foundation date. Recent work has done much to clarify our ideas on the emergence of town life in Britain,[31] but what of towns excavated long ago, or sites with limited investigation or ones with only casual finds? Caerwent, for instance, has yielded much Flavian pottery,[32] but it is questionable whether a town can be claimed at that period, since the pottery might be derived from a military site and its attendant *vicus*. Certainly the published evidence demonstrates that the rampart is not Flavian as used to be claimed[33] and it cannot in fact be earlier than A.D. 130.[34] Exeter is another town where the same question may be put. Pre-Flavian development of a town among the Dumnonii might not be impossible, though it would be mildly surprising. Yet Exeter has produced Claudian samian, including stamps from dies represented at Valkenburg in Periods I and II.[35] It is difficult to believe that they could have got there unless the occupants of the excavated areas were in close touch with a source of army supplies. Much the same applies, though with less evidence, at Dorchester, Dorset,[36] and in the north at Aldborough. Does the undoubted Flavian pottery at the latter mean the beginning of the town proper,[37] or is it really the beginning of the town as satellite of a fort that we are seeing hinted? The second alternative seems likelier on the face of things, particularly as a fort is to be expected here on the general pattern of the military network. But the dating evidence divorced from structures will never settle the point.

As a final exercise it is perhaps worth considering again the matter of town defences. Mr Wacher deals elsewhere with second-century earthworks (p. 60), but the hoary problem of the walls remains pressing. Lack of evidence is a common feature of the situation in many towns. For others we have recently had vivid reminders of the need to have as many sections as possible in dealing with this aspect of dating. Towns with only one or two published sections whose walls have been dated earlier than the closing years of the second century are now clearly suspect. At least we may now be sure that some town walls were built very much later than used to be thought.[38] Cursory re-examination of published evidence suggests two more unlikely to be earlier than the mid-third century.[39] And London, with a worn coin of A.D. 183-4 below the thickening of the fort wall,[40] presumed reasonably enough to be contemporary with the town defence, is perhaps a likely candidate. Lincoln, too, is a site that may need further consideration.[41]

It is abundantly clear that Dr Corder's thesis of construction of town walls under Clodius Albinus[42] is no longer tenable in simple all-embracing form. One wonders what re-examination of the sherds from unpublished or incompletely published sections of the defences of other towns would reveal. Investigation of these is now an urgent matter. Perhaps the truth of the matter is that we have been too anxious to read into our evidence neat schemes which would provide general justification of grants of murage at a specific time whether under Albinus,[42] or the Severi.[43] As matters stand, it is not easy to believe that either Aldborough, with *termini post et ante quos* implying Severan construction at the latest,[44] or Great Casterton, with so many sections widely separated giving a late second-century *terminus post quem*[45] can be placed in the same category as some of the towns mentioned above.

As for the future, it is at least possible to claim that our understanding of secondary sources of dating-evidence is gradually improving and so is the diligence with which our excavators are applying the results and publishing them with adequate presentation of the evidence. Many perplexing problems remain, but the auguries are favourable.

NOTES

[1] Suetonius, *divus Titus*, iv, 1.

[2] *S.H.A., vita Hadriani*, xi, 2.

[3] Ammianus Marcellinus, xxviii, 3, 2.

[4] P. Corder, *Arch.J.*, cxii, 41, tentatively suggested a connexion with Constans' visit in A.D. 343, but later evidence showed that one bastion was built in or after A.D. 354 (*Great Casterton*, III, 28). J. P. C. Kent then suggested a possible context in the arrival of Lupicinus in Britain in A.D. 360 (*ibid.*, 29). Absence of destruction that can be assigned to A.D. 367 from our towns does not carry automatic conviction that they had already modernized their defences, particularly since we have little notion of what did happen in the civil areas then.

[5] Tacitus, *Agricola*, xxi.

[6] *Antiq.J.*, xxxvi, 8.

[7] Clearly the time taken to erect public buildings must have varied greatly. We can be specific about the elaborate Forum at Lepcis Magna, at least five years: J. B. Ward Perkins, *J.R.S.*, xxxviii, 64, with a reference to *Africa Italica*, ii, 231-45. In Britain in the Flavian period skilled labour would not readily be available, except in the legions, and the legions had other matters in hand.

[8] D. Atkinson. *Excavations at Wroxeter 1923-7*, 177.

9 P. Corder and T. Romans, *Excavations at the Roman Town at Brough-Petuaria 1937,* 61 ff.

10 *C.I.L.,* vii, 11.

11 *B.B.C.S.,* xv, 83.

12 So A. L. F. Rivet, *Town and Country in Roman Britain* (1958), 24.

13 No estimate of wear is given for the coin dating the bastion at Great Casterton already mentioned. The same applies to the vital coins dating the first destruction of the Wroxeter Forum including the latest ones of A.D. 155 (D. Atkinson, *op. cit.,* 105). It may be well to record that in conversation with the writer the late Professor Donald Atkinson's recollection was that the two coins were 'worn, but not very worn'. A minimum life of five to ten years in circulation may be postulated.

14 Recent improvements in the dating of fourth-century coins should help here. See R. A. G. Carson, P. V. Hill, and J. P. C. Kent, *Late Roman Bronze Coins 324-498* (Spink, 1960).

15 A wall in Yorkshire, probably nineteenth-century, is now 'dated' to A.D. 1959 or later by a coin inserted into a chink in its footings and pushed, with the aid of a stick, into its foundations by a small boy. Gaps between floorboards notoriously attract attention from the young.

16 R. Knorr's fundamental works, *Töpfer und Fabriken verzierter Terra-sigillata des ersten Jahrhunderts* (1919) and *Terra-sigillata-Gefässe des ersten Jahrhunderts mit Töpfernamen* (1952) are invaluable for identification, but much supplementary evidence has to be taken into account. The Boudiccan burning at Colchester, the divided occupation at Valkenburg, and material from the military sites in Germany and Scotland are especially important. A study of samian from military sites thought to have been evacuated when Hadrian's Wall was built suggests that regular import from South Gaul continued to at least A.D. 110, as indeed the late Donald Atkinson always held. Most early Central Gaulish exports came from the kilns at Les Martres de Veyre (*Germania,* xxxii, 171; *Revue archéologique du Centre,* II, 261 ff; *Gallia,* xxi, 227-39): it is now evident that serious export from Lezoux only began in the middle of Hadrian's reign.

17 Little samian from such sites has been published. Newstead (*P.S.A.S.,* lxxxiv, 27-31) and Corbridge (partial publication in *Arch.Ael.,* 4, xxxi, 242-53) stand almost alone.

18 Such sites as Brough-on-Noe, reoccupied after a long gap c. A.D. 158. There are many other northern forts obviously with similar histories, but as this is deduced from the samian, it is impossible to use the evidence from these forts in dating other sites by samian without becoming involved in circular argument.

19 At the University of Leeds. Publication will take a long time; meanwhile any available information on particular dies will gladly be made available to inquirers.

20 M. H. Callender, *Arch.Ael.,* 4, xxvii, 60-121. Publication of Dr Callender's Durham thesis will give a wider survey soon.

21 I am indebted to Monsieur Hughes Vertèt for his opinion on this matter.

22 *Revue archéologique,* I, 360-394 and Déchelette, *Vases ornés de la Gaule romaine,* I, 41 for St. Rémy-en-Rollat (Allier). E. M. Jope, *A.N.L.,* 2, No. 12, 199 for British products.

23 *Cf.* types 44-48 in J. P. Gillam, *Types of Roman Coarse Pottery Vessels in Northern Britain* (1957), offprinted from *Arch.Ael.,* 4, xxxv. Import in connexion with East Gaulish samian is perhaps possible.

24 B. R. Hartley, *Notes on the Roman Pottery Industry in the Nene Valley.* Peterborough Museum (1960).

25 M. R. Hull, *The Roman Potters' Kilns of Colchester* (1963) *passim.*

26 Around A.D. 150-160, though quite possibly with local distribution predominating at first.

27 J. P. Gillam, *op.cit.* This is now out of print: a plea for reprinting, if possible with revision, would be widely echoed.

28 For fuller discussion of some of the points involved, *Archaeometry,* v, 1-3.

29 Wroxeter is a clear case in point; Leicester scarcely less so — *Jewry Wall, passim.*

30 Mortimer Wheeler, *Roman Art and Architecture* (1964), 204.

31 Canterbury, Verulamium, and Cirencester notably.

32 *Arch.,* lxxx, pl. lxxxiv.

33 *Ibid.,* S 96, from the primary bank, is not earlier than A.D. 130 and may well be Antonine. The published photograph does not show the ovolo clearly enough.

34 *Ibid.,* 274.

35 Stamps of PRIMVS, MODESTVS, and NIGER are from dies recorded in Periods I and II at Valkenburg (i.e. A.D. 43-48 according to van Giffen).

36 An early stamp of AQVINTANVS in the Museum, for instance. The Dorchester samian has not been re-examined thoroughly, however.

37 *Y.A.J.* xl, 1-77, *passim.*

38 E.g. Canterbury, A.D. 270-290 (Sheppard Frere, *Roman Canterbury,* 3rd ed., 10); Great Chesterford, probably fourth-century (*V.C.H. Essex,* iii, 75-6); Mancetter, late third- or early fourth-century (*T.B.A.S.,* lxxiv, 39); Dorchester-on-Thames, after A.D. 250 (*Arch. J.,* cxix, 130).

39 Namely Silchester and Caerwent. At the former the evidence was admirably published, and with due caution, by Mrs Cotton (*Arch.,* xcii, 121 ff.). It would be surprising if the colour-coated beakers of fig. 15, nos. 12 and 13, were earlier than the middle of the third century. The Caerwent evidence seems unequivocally in favour of a date after A.D. 240, since the rampart contemporary with the wall yielding black-burnished dishes of Gillam type 227 (A.D. 240-320 according to Gillam), as well as third-century black-burnished jars (*Arch.,* lxxx, fig. 13, C10, C28, C44, and C46). Some caution is needed perhaps, because there is evidence elsewhere in the circuit of pits cut into the secondary rampart: but the very fact that they were seen elsewhere is comforting.

40 *J.R.S.,* xlvii, 220.

41 *Arch. J.,* cxvii, fig. 7, 14 apparently has the characteristic third-century groove around the top of the flange, as in Gillam types 226-7, but the base sags in a manner not typical of those forms, and the piece may be a sport. A firm *terminus post quem* of A.D. 181 is given by a worn coin with 'wear consistent with a life of some twenty years' (R. A. G. Carson). Severan walling is perhaps possible or even likely here, then, as Mr D. F. Petch suggested, but it is worth noting in passing that much of the Lincoln pottery has a local flavour and is obviously difficult to date at all closely. Mr Petch points out to me that colour-coated ware is absent from pre-wall groups, however.

42 With Dr Corder, *Arch. J.,* cxii, 124.

43 With A. L. F. Rivet, *Town and Country in Roman Britain* (1958), 83.

44 *Y.A.J.,* xl, 64-8.

45 *Great Casterton,* II, 1 ff.

EARTHWORK DEFENCES OF THE SECOND CENTURY
by
J. S. Wacher

THE paper delivered to the Conference was based on one which has since appeared in the *Archaeological Journal,* volume cxix (1964). Consequently only a short summary is here included of what has already appeared in print, and the reader is referred to the original version for points requiring amplification. But since that article was written, some fresh evidence has come to light and some new suggestions can be made, and these are discussed more fully.

The original paper made no mention of the structural features of these ramparts, and these are described first. The majority of ramparts are of *glacis* type, and so far no evidence for timber revetments either at front or rear has been found. Sometimes turf or clay cheeks are used to retain the rampart core, as at Cirencester,[1] and occasionally it is constructed throughout of turf, like that of Period IV at Brough-on-Humber.[2] The core frequently contains occupation debris as well as clay and turf, scraped up from the surface inside the line of the bank, as at Verulamium.[3] The full width of the rampart is often difficult to determine, as in so many cases the front has been cut back for the insertion of the stone wall at a later date. The Fosse at Verulamium was 52 ft wide where it remained undisturbed by the wall,[4] but this great width seems exceptional, and an estimated width of 15 ft for the rampart at Cirencester, based on its relation to the Verulamium Gate, would appear more normal.[5] On rare occasions, for instance, at Dorchester-on-Thames, timber lacing seems to have been used to give added support where the bank passed over unstable ground.[6]

Slight evidence for interval towers constructed of timber comes from Cirencester, where at one point a massive beam had been inserted in, and parallel to, the rampart, close to its rear face.[7] It may be inferred that a similar beam would have occupied a position near the front face, and the two together could then have acted as the base plates for a tower of light construction. Such towers almost certainly existed at Lincoln after the legionary defences had been remodelled for the *colonia*.[8]

Little is known about the construction of the gates connected with these ramparts. North and West gates of timber certainly existed at Brough-on-Humber,[9] but in most cases the evidence for them will have been destroyed when they were replaced by stone gates.

At Cirencester, however, the rampart is stratigraphically later than the stone-built Verulamium Gate, although both probably belong to the same chronological period.[10] With this in mind, a strong case could be made for the

FORTIFIED TOWNS

▲ ALDBOROUGH

△ YORK

■ BROUGH

CAISTOR

LINCOLN
■
    HORNCASTLE

△ BROUGH

THORPE □
      ▲ ANCASTER
■ ROCESTER   CASTLE HILL

WROXETER   LEICESTER   ▲ GT. CASTERTON   CAISTER
■   ▲ WALL   ▲   □
       MANCETTER   △ WATER NEWTON   CAISTER

DROITWICH △   CHESTERTON   ▲ GODMANCHESTER
           ▲   IRCHESTER   △ CAMBRIDGE
   ▲ ALCESTER   ▲ TOWCESTER
■ KENCHESTER   ▲ GT. CHESTERFORD
    △ DORN   △ BRAUGHING   ▲ COLCHESTER
■ GLOUCESTER   □ ALCHESTER
                   ■ VERULAMIUM
CAERWENT   CIRENCESTER   ■ DORCHESTER
                     ▲ LONDON
BATH ■   □   ROCHESTER
      MILDENHALL   ■ SILCHESTER   CANTERBURY

            ■ WINCHESTER
■ ILCHESTER   BITTERNE
                CHICHESTER
■ EXETER   DORCHESTER
        ■

                   ▲ WITHOUT EARLY RAMPARTS
                   ■ WITH   "   "
                   □ NOT PROVED
                   △ NO EVIDENCE

Fig. 10. Fortified towns.

re-examination of certain other similar gates in some Romano-British towns, notably at Verulamium and Silchester. At Verulamium, Sir Mortimer Wheeler noted that the town wall was built from a higher level than the gate tower of the Chester Gate, and over-rode the offsets, although he concluded that both belonged to the same structural period.[11] Since Verulamium is a town which was provided with second-century earthwork defences,[12] it is possible that both London and Chester Gates belong to this phase. Both gates lie on the line or probable line of the Fosse, in marked contrast to the differently planned Silchester Gate,[13] which does not.

At Silchester the only indication that perhaps all is not as it seems is given in the excavation report of 1908 on the East Gate, by Mr St John Hope. Quoting from this source it is found that "they showed that on the north the gateway was built up with a straight joint against the inner face of the wall, which overlapped it for a distance of 4 ft 8 in. But the gateway was not quite parallel with the wall and on the south the rubble of the wall had been cut away to a depth of 14 in to allow the south-east corner of the gateway to be recessed into it."[14] A re-examination of this point might reveal much.

The towns now shown to have possessed second-century earthwork defences may be stated, together with a summary of dates : Exeter, with a *terminus post quem* of the second quarter of the second century;[15] Ilchester with one of about A.D. 90, although here a reassessment may prove it later;[16] Dorchester (Dorset), with one of A.D. 140;[17] Caerwent, probably Hadrianic or later;[18] Cirencester, at least as late as A.D. 140-50 and probably later;[19] Dorchester-on-Thames, dated by Professor Frere to A.D. 185;[20] Silchester to about A.D. 160;[21] Winchester, not yet dated satisfactorily;[22] Clausentum, almost certainly defended during the later second century, although the exact line cannot yet be determined with certainty;[23] Chichester, dated to the late second century;[24] Rochester to about A.D. 150-60;[25] the Fosse earthwork at Verulamium, apparently left incomplete and now shown to date to the second century;[26] Kenchester, with a *terminus post quem* of A.D. 140;[27] Wroxeter with one of A.D. 150 or later;[28] Brough-on-Humber, with its two periods of second-century earthwork, the latest dated to the period after A.D. 150;[29] Caister-by-Yarmouth with its palisade dated to the Hadrianic period;[30] Bath dated to the second half of the second century;[31] and Rocester to not earlier than A.D. 160.[32] To this list must be added Lincoln[33] and Gloucester,[34] where at both places the legionary defences were probably refurbished for use by the early *coloniae*.

There are also some doubtful cases where the existence of earthworks has not yet been proved beyond reasonable doubt. Most of these cases, for Colchester,[35] Caistor-by-Norwich,[36] Mildenhall,[37] and Alchester[38] have already been argued in the earlier article, but some additional comments on Mancetter may not come amiss. Here, there is an earlier ditch underlying the later stone-wall rampart, which the excavator considered to have been closed by about A.D. 120, which is a little early for the present discussion.[39] But he also observed what was called 'two-stage robbing' of the wall, with the inner face being robbed before the core, giving rise to two vertical cuts in front of the rampart.[40] Robbing of this type is by no means impossible, but it is perhaps a point worthy of re-exami-

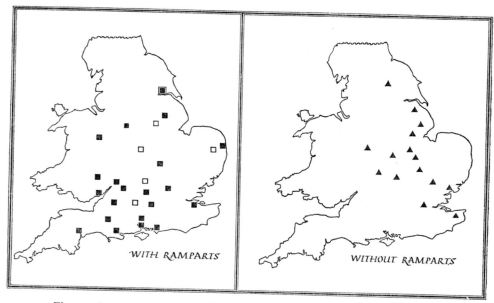

Fig. 11. Comparative distributions of towns with and without earth ramparts.

nation.[41] To this list of doubtful cases must also be added Thorpe-by-Newark, as the result of excavations in 1963,[42] and Irchester.[43]

Of the towns not provided with earthwork defences, Canterbury,[44] Aldborough,[45] and Great Casterton[46] must be considered as well-attested examples. Apart from these, no sign of such earthworks has yet been found at Leicester,[47] Ancaster,[48] Caistor (Lincs.),[49] Horncastle,[50] Wall,[51] Towcester,[52] Water Newton,[53] Godmanchester,[54] Chesterton-on-Fosse,[55] and Great Chesterford,[56] although in no case has sufficient work been done for certainty.

Lastly, so little is known of the defences at Alcester, Droitwich, Cambridge, Dorn, Brough (Notts.), and Braughing, that no conclusions of any sort can be made.

To sum up the evidence. Certain towns appear to have been provided with defences of an earthwork type, probably during the second half of the second century, if the dating evidence has been correctly assessed. In one case, and possibly in two others, these earthworks were used in conjunction with large stone-built gates of defensive character. Certain other towns do not seem to have been provided with such defences and at least one instance—Canterbury —was probably not defended at all before the end of the third century. Two other points must be considered, that of geographical distribution and that of status. Geographically, defended towns lie predominantly in the south and west of England, with one or two outliers on, or close to, the east coast (Figs. 10 & 11).

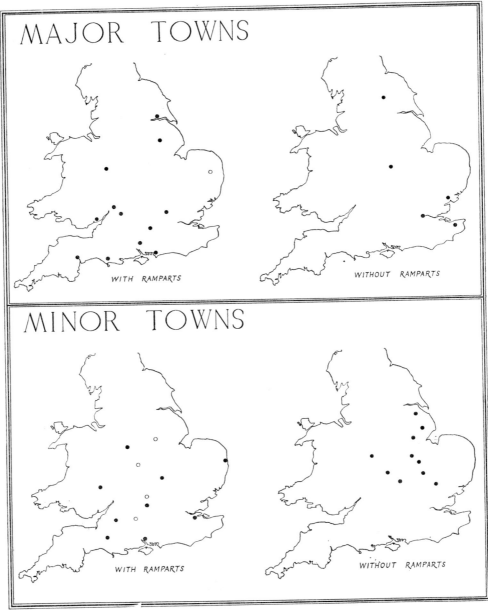

Fig. 12. Comparative distributions, according to size, of towns with and without earth ramparts.

The south-west is the area containing statistically most cantonal capitals and it might be argued that the banks are the prerogative of such towns and reflect their status. But an analysis of towns in the two regions according to status shows that this is not so. Reference to Fig. 12 shows that both major and minor towns possess earthwork defences and each class can be broadly separated into two mutually exclusive groups. The legal position of towns desiring to erect defences in the later second century is defined in the Digest[57] and its application to the present problems has been discussed in the earlier account.

The structural evidence for these earthworks is reasonably clear, but the explanation for their existence is not, and it remains to examine their purpose and the historical events, if any, which may have caused their erection.

Civic pride has sometimes been cited as a motive for town-wall building, but it is less likely to have been operative in the case of earthworks. That apart, two other reasons present themselves. In the first place they may have been provided to delimit the town boundaries and so channel all entry and exit through the gates, in which case permission would have to be sought for their erection; if granted, the resulting banks would ease the collection of dues and the control of traffic, and might be thought in time to have acquired a symbolic value indicative of status. But this can hardly be the reason for their construction, since there are inconsistencies; Canterbury and Aldborough, both cantonal capitals, were not provided with ramparts, yet they were built around small towns like Kenchester and Dorchester-on-Thames. Neither does there seem any good reason to explain why towns in the south and west should be given visible boundaries, while most of those in the east did without them. So it would seem that this motive for the building of earth ramparts cannot be considered seriously at present.

The second reason for their construction gives rise to a choice of premises. If they were primarily defensive in character, as seems likely, they could have been erected for reasons of economy, being initially much cheaper than permanent works in stone, although subsequent cost of upkeep may well have been greater. But this does not provide the reasons for their construction; it would only explain the choice of material used. Neither can it be said that at a certain time a general ordinance was issued for the fortification of all towns in Britain, in which some chose stone walls and others earth banks, because it is known that Canterbury, at least, remained undefended until the stone wall was built towards the end of the third century. Therefore it might be concluded that the towns which possessed earth ramparts were fortified at some specified time, while others were not and had to wait until later, so that there is a clear-cut division into two classes.

The second premise arising from this consideration of their defensive character, is that they were built in an emergency, which seems at the moment to be the most probable explanation. There is, however, a difficulty in accepting it, for at Cirencester and possibly also at Verulamium and Silchester, the ramparts are related in time with massive stone-built gates,[58] and it would be unlikely that a programme of urgent fortification would be interrupted and delayed while such gates were built. So that, if these ramparts are genuine emergency measures, it implies that the gates were already in existence when work started on them, and any explanation must therefore be comprehensive enough to take this into account. These gates might possibly have been built as free-standing monumental structures to mark the limits of the towns along the main roads leading into them, and to provide suitably impressive entrances at these points on the boundaries. But the character of the gates would appear to be against such a hypothesis, for their nature is clearly defensive. Could they, therefore, have been part of a more ambitious scheme of fortification in stone, which, for certain reasons, did not at once materialize? Some such scheme may have been envisaged at Cirencester, where the Verulamium Gate is contemporary with the bridge outside it. A bridge implies that it was the intention to divert the river from its original course through the middle of the town to run outside the defences, and this would be a logical action only if it was intended to build a wall or some other sort of fortification around the town.

The following tentative suggestions may therefore be made. Is it possible that at some time during the later second century, and in the face of a sustained threat from one of the frontiers, certain towns in Britain received orders to erect fortifications? At first the threat may not have been very serious, with the work being planned entirely in stone. The gates may have been built at first with the ultimate intention of linking them by a curtain wall, when perhaps the vague threat was suddenly transformed into outright danger, requiring immediate measures to be taken. The timely erection of a bank and ditch round the town, taking in such gates as had already been built, would be an obvious solution. The incompleteness of the Fosse Earthwork at Verulamium might in turn suggest that the immediate danger was perhaps not so very serious and soon passed. At a convenient time, and it may not have been immediately convenient, return could be made to the original plans, and these temporary fortifications could be rebuilt in more durable materials. It is interesting to observe, therefore, that where this occurred within a reasonable space of time, perhaps twenty to thirty years, the stone walls usually occupied the same alignment as the earlier earthworks, which would provide a convenient line and backing. But where stone walls were not added until much later, perhaps not before the fourth century, the line was sometimes changed, as at Mildenhall, presumably because in these cases the bank and ditch had become obscured.

When did this threat arise, if the defences were erected on account of a threat from one of the frontiers? The latest date yet ascribed to any one of these ramparts is A.D. 185, for that at Dorchester-on-Thames, and a number of others can be placed firmly into the second half of the second century. So it would have been some time towards the end of that century, and certainly after A.D. 180.

More important perhaps, where did the threat originate? A series of revolts or invasions took place in the north of Britain during the second half of the second century, culminating in the barbarian invasion of A.D. 196-7. It must not be overlooked that Dr Corder put forward a suggestion relating the building of stone walls to the usurpation of Clodius Albinus,[59] but it would now appear that the dating evidence for some town walls is too late to fit this context. Consequently, the invasion of A.D. 196 must now be considered as being a possible cause of our earth ramparts. But its seriousness has perhaps been overestimated in the past and it is now reasonably certain that the Vale of York did not suffer from this invasion;[60] and those that came before it would seem to be either too early or not widespread enough to warrant such measures being taken so far south. The absence of defences at Canterbury might be explained by its distance from the seat of any invasion or revolt in the north, but the same explanation will clearly not do to account for their presence at the equally remote towns of Exeter or Ilchester, and their apparent absence at the nearer town of Aldborough.

It is necessary, therefore, to look for a satisfactory explanation elsewhere and the clue to this might be given by the geographical distribution of the fortified towns (Fig. 11). Of the two distinct groups, the one in the south and west is the larger and may suggest that, at some time during the latter part of the second century, unrest or possibly outright revolt occurred among the Welsh tribes, or even among the Dumnonii of the south-west peninsula. But until a great deal more evidence has been collected, the nature of this unrest and its exact focus cannot be clearly determined. The suggestion is, however, to some extent supported by the recently revised views on the Roman military occupation of Wales.[61]

The finding of an early third-century inscription at the Saxon Shore fort of Reculver[62] implies that the east coast was becoming unsafe at a much earlier date than has been up-to-now accepted. It is possible therefore that the three towns on the east coast, where the presence of earthworks has been proved, may belong to the early stages of coastal fortification.

But whatever tentative conclusions are drawn from the evidence, it must be clear that much more is required before these conclusions can be accepted as more than hypothesis. In considering problems related to town defences, it is as well not to lose sight of the towns as a whole, and careful study of internal buildings may provide clues to the proper understanding of the fortifications. This is particularly true where alignments have changed, and excavation in the areas enclosed between the earthworks and later stone walls at both Verulamium and Caistor-by-Norwich, might provide more satisfactory dating evidence than several sections cut across their respective lines. It is also worth remembering that some of the smaller towns, such as Caistor (Lincs.) and Horncastle, may not have been fortified during the second century because there was nothing worth defending, and only extensive excavations inside such towns will provide the answer.

NOTES

1 *Antiq. J.*, xliv, pl. xix.
2 *Ibid.*, xl, 62.
3 *Verulamium*, pl. xviii; *Antiquity*, xxxviii, 103; *Bull. Inst. Arch.*, iv, 69.
4 *Ibid.*
5 *Antiq. J.*, xli, 64.
6 *Arch. J.*, cxix, 118.
7 *Antiq. J.*, xliv, 16.
8 *Roman Lincoln*, 9; *Arch. J.*, cxvii, 54.
9 *Antiq. J.*, xl, 64.
10 *Ibid.*, xli, 65.
11 *Verulamium*, 68.
12 *loc.cit.*
13 *Ibid.*, 71.
14 *Arch.*, lxi, 475.
15 A. Fox, *Roman Exeter*, 19; *J.R.S.*, lii, 184.
16 *J.R.S.*, xxxix, 108; xl, 110.
17 *Ibid.*, xlii, 99; xlvi, 142; *P.D.N.H.S.*, lxxv, 72; lxxvii, 128.
18 *Arch.*, lxxx, 268; *Antiq. J.*, xxxviii, 4*n*.
19 *Antiq. J.*, xliv, 16.
20 *Arch. J.*, cxix, 118.
21 *Arch.*, xcii, 121.
22 *P.H.F.C.*, xxii, 57.
23 M. A. Cotton and P. W. Gathercole, *Excavations at Clausentum, 1951-4*, 34; *J.R.S.*, l, 233.
24 *Suss.A.C.*, c, 86 ff.
25 *Arch.Cant.*, lxxvi, p. lxxiv.
26 *Bull.Inst.Arch.*, iv, 69.
27 *T.Wool.N.F.C.*, xxxv, 138.
28 *T.Shrop.A.S.*, lvii, 125; *T.B.A.S.*, lxxviii, 31.
29 *Antiq. J.*, xl, 62.
30 *J.R.S.*, xlii; 96; *Norf.Arch.*, xxxiii, 94.
31 Information from Mr B. Cunliffe.
32 *N.Staffs.J. of F.S.*, ii, 41.
33 *Arch.J.*, cxvii, 54.
34 *T.B.G.A.S.*, lxxxi, 10 ff.
35 *Roman Colchester*, fig. 18, 22.
36 *J.R.S.*, li, 132.
37 *J.R.S.*, xliii, 90; *W.A.M.*, lvi, 241.
38 *Antiq.J.*, ix, 105; xii, 36.
39 *T.B.A.S.*, lxxiv, 30.
40 *Ibid.*, fig. 4.
41 Miss C. Mahany undertook further excavations in 1964, close to the east gate. No evidence for a two-stage robbing of the wall, or of an early rampart was obtained.
42 *J.R.S.*, liv, 159.
43 Information from Mr J. Knight.
44 S. S. Frere, *Roman Canterbury*, (3rd ed.), 10.
45 *Y.A.J.*, xl, 1 ff.
46 *Great Casterton*, II, 1.
47 *J.R.S.*, xlix, 113.
48 *Ibid.*, xlvii, 210; li, 171; lii, 167.
49 *Antiq. J.*, xl, 187.
50 *Arch. J.*, ciii, 22.
51 *T.A.B.S.*, lxxv, 25; *J.R.S.*, lii, 170.
52 *J.R.S.*, xlv, 135.

53 *Ibid.*, xlviii, 139.
54 *P.Camb.Ant.S.*, liv, 76.
55 *J.R.S.*, lii, 171.
56 *Ibid.*, xi, 106.
57 *Digest,* I, viii; 9, 4 (Ulpian); *ibid.*, I, x; 6 (Modestinus).
58 Cf. pp. 60-2.
59 *Arch. J.*, cxii, 20 ff.
60 *P.Leeds Phil. and Lit.S.*, ix, 118.
61 *B.B.C.S.*, xx, 206 ff; *Arch.Camb.*, cxi, 103 ff; cxii, 13 ff.
62 *Antiq. J.*, xli, 224.

LEGAL AND CONSTITUTIONAL PROBLEMS
by
Joyce M. Reynolds

THERE is so little evidence for the organization of local government in
Roman Britain that historians have perforce to turn to the municipal
system of Italy and the other Western provinces of the Roman Empire
for a model from which to draw a picture of the kind of way in which it will
have worked.

In broad outline, Western society was based on towns, each the centre of a
territorium, each equipped with institutions through which its citizens enjoyed a
measure of local self-government under Roman supervision. Towns were graded
in privilege—colonies of Roman citizens at the top of the scale, then *municipia*
of Roman citizens, then communities of Latin status (at first called colonies,
later, more often, *municipia*) and finally communities of peregrine status.
Colonies and *municipia,* whether of Roman or Latin status, were organized on
a standard pattern derived from Rome itself and their institutions were established and defined in charters authorized by the central government: they are
called chartered towns in what follows. Peregrine communities were organized
on the basis of their native traditions, with modifications derived from Roman
practice. Below the level of the towns there were also, where appropriate, subordinate units—*pagi* in rural areas and *vici* in minor built-up ones— which
possessed some local organization, though of a less developed kind than that of
the towns. There were also some groups which had no recognized institutions
of their own, being thought either too small, too scattered or too poor to sustain
them, or too barbarous to accept the idea of self-discipline within the Roman
framework; these came wholly under the control of the nearest town or of an
imperial official.[1]

In detail, the most relevant parallels for British affairs should be found in
the Gallic areas where pre-Roman society was organized in tribes, as in Britain.[2]
In these, strategic considerations sometimes led to the elimination of particular
tribes as political entities, but the norm was to preserve them as units of local
government centred on their old tribal capitals. Their administration seems to
have been carried on through councils and magistrates, who might at first retain
their old titles but eventually adopted the nearest Latin equivalent,[3] which had
the advantage of being readily understood by the newest freshman on the governor's staff. With the modification of nomenclature there may well have gone
modification of function, which brought them more into line with the magistrates of Italian-type communities. Their institutions remained, however,
those of peregrines, unless, for good reason, they were deemed to have earned
promotion. In Gallia Narbonensis, Julius Caesar decided that substantially all
tribesmen deserved such promotion, and he managed this by giving their tribal
capitals the status of Latin cities and enrolling the tribesmen as citizens of these

newly-chartered towns. As a result, tribal government and traditions gave way to civic government and to traditions derived from Italy; while the annual magistrates of the cities, together with their families, acquired full Roman citizenship at the end of their years of office. Among the justifications for this was the economic prosperity of the province and the spread of Roman influence throughout its countryside by immigrants from Italy, some of them voluntary, some official settlers. Further north, immigration on this scale did not occur and, perhaps, prosperity was not so evenly spread. Some tribal areas never seem to have made the grade for promotion; in others, the towns developed promisingly, while the countryside remained comparatively backward. What might happen then can be illustrated from the territory of the Helvetii. Their tribal capital of Aventicum, a prosperous road-centre and market, which was strongly Romanized, achieved promotion to be a colony under the Flavians; but the more backward country-dwelling tribesmen remained peregrine.[4] This entailed a complicated administrative system—major matters of local government were dealt with by the colonial magistrates, minor ones by the officers of the many flourishing *vici* which emerged in the country districts; but for some purposes the old tribal institutions seem to have been maintained, centred on the old tribal capital at Aventicum, where the *civitas Helvetiorum* continued to set up monuments to emperors and patrons alongside those of the colony. It is probable that, legally, the peregrine tribesmen were *attributi* of the colony, i.e. tax-paying dependents, and one may also guess that such men, drifting into the town from the country, formed a high percentage of the group known as the *incolae* at Aventicum, i.e. residents in the town who were not on its citizen roll. A similar situation can be glimpsed elsewhere, e.g. at Langres, where inscriptions refer both to a *civitas Lingonum* and to a *colonia Lingonum*.[5]

There were also occasions when the Romans introduced citizen settlers into a tribal area, taking land from the tribesmen and establishing a colony over their heads. The position of such tribesmen varied according to circumstances. The intransigent and defeated sub-Alpine tribe of the Salassi in North Italy seem to have lost all independent organization and have survived only as the *attributi* of the colony of citizen settlers at Aosta;[6] the civilized and co-operative Atacini of Southern France appear to have been enrolled in the citizen-body of the colony at Narbonne;[7] the partly-civilized and co-operative tribe of the Ubii in Western Germany survived as the *civitas Ubiorum* alongside the settlers in the colony at Cologne, where tribesmen and colonists intermingled happily and fruitfully, producing a social picture not in fact unlike that at Aventicum.[8]

But did anything precisely like this happen in Roman Britain? It seems to me desirable to approach the problem in Britain without expecting to find that the British tribes were uniformly organized, much less uniformly privileged. It is indeed improbable that they were uniformly organized before the Romans came; and since the Romans were, by tradition, tolerant of what they found in new territory, usually willing to allow its survival unless it was clearly unserviceable, they are unlikely to have imposed uniformity in place of a variety which worked. Moreover the conquest of Britain was by stages. Some tribes not immediately annexed, underwent, nevertheless, strong Roman influence; and by the time they were annexed may well have modified their institutions by imitation. At the same time what one generation of conquerors deemed service-able and retained might not always appeal to its successors, who might abolish it everywhere or might retain it where it had received official approval in the past but abolish it when it turned up among newly-conquered groups. Claudius retained a king among the Regnenses, but kings are not attested among other annexed groups in his time and there is no evidence that monarchy survived even at Regnum in a later period.[9] And not only is it likely that variety is what the Romans found, retained, and refined upon according to their own changing ideas, but also that under their rule particular communities underwent the processes of Romanization in different degrees according to their geographical proximity to Roman influences, to their own psychology, and to their economic ability to afford Roman manners. Some will have gone much further than others in voluntary or unconscious modification of their traditional practices; and it would be entirely in line with Roman policy to reward these, and only these, with promotion.

The basic fact known about local organization in Roman Britain is that many tribes did survive as corporate bodies. Tribal self-consciousness is attested in those inscriptions in which a man or woman gives a tribal rather than a civic origin—as *civis Cantius*,[10] *civis Dobunnus*;[11] tribal activity in those recording working-parties on Hadrian's Wall—*civitas Catuvellaunorum*,[12] *civitas Dumnoniorum*,[13] and, probably, *civitas Durotrigum*;[14] tribal administration in those of the *civitas Cornoviorum* at Wroxeter,[15] the *civitas Silurum* at Caerwent,[16] and perhaps the *civitas Dobunnorum* at Kenchester.[17] At Wroxeter and Caerwent the administration is attested actually in the tribal capitals; and it is a fair assumption that there was a similar administration in all those tribal capitals which, like these two, are listed in the Itineraries and by the Ravenna Geographer with a tribal name in the genitive following the town-name[18]—as Venta Icenorum, Venta Belgarum—and therefore that the normal unit of local government in Britain was the tribe rather than the town; the tribe with its governmental institutions based on the tribal capital.

What do we know about those institutions? In pre-Roman Britain it appears that the tribe was governed by a chief or king and/or a council of nobles. Apart from the notorious Cogidubnus among the Regnenses[19] there is no evidence that kings survived annexation; and a possible continental parallel—the *summus magistratus* among the Batavi[20]—is less significant than it might be since the Batavi were technically federate, not subject. The Romans had a penchant for oligarchy as against monarchy and one would expect their influence to be exerted accordingly—that is certainly what happened in France—and in conformity with expectation we find that the Cornovii acted on the decree of their *ordo,* i.e. their council (they must have had magistrates too, but of these we hear nothing). *Ordo* may mean the *ordo decurionum* or town-council of a chartered community; but it is also often used to describe the corresponding body in any corporation, even a burial club. It implies nothing certainly about the status of the community of the Cornovii—only that they had an institution which could be described by this Latin word and an oligarchic organization. In fact the formulae used and the tribal activities recorded at Wroxeter, at Caerwent, and, if you accept the *C.I.L.* reading, on the Kenchester milestone, suggest strongly that, at the time when those inscriptions were cut, there was no chartered community among the Cornovii, the Silures and the Dobunni, but that their tribal organizations, being necessarily of peregrine status, provided the overriding local administration in their territories.[21]

On the other hand, there is a little evidence to suggest that some tribal capitals had perhaps been promoted, were chartered, and possessed civic institutions which overshadowed the tribal organization if that survived. Thus an auxiliary soldier named Novanticus, who fought in Trajan's Dacian Wars, described himself as a man of Ratae, not as *civis Coritanus*,[21] and it may well be right to deduce from this that Leicester had a municipal life that counted for more in the eyes of its citizens than membership of the tribe of the Coritani, and was probably, therefore, chartered. If, on one of the inscriptions of the *collegium peregrinorum* at Silchester, we were to follow Haverfield's suggestion that the letters C. C. could be resolved as *civitatis Callevensium*,[22] the conclusion would be even clearer for Silchester; but it has to be admitted that the second text[23] points rather to their resolution as *consistentium Callevae,* a phrase which is uninformative for our purposes. And there is Verulamium. I am one of those who believe that Tacitus meant what he said when he described Verulamium as a *municipium*, i.e. that it was a chartered town, though whether with Latin or with full Roman status we do not know, already in the first century A.D.[24] If so, we have a British tribe with a history not unlike that of the Helvetii—its tribal capital promoted but its tribal organization surviving in some sense (for we have that later reference to the *civitas Catuvellaunorum* as a working-party on Hadrian's Wall), essentially, I suppose, for the country tribesmen who are unlikely to have appeared sufficiently advanced to be enrolled among the citizens of the *municipium*. My guess would be that the Romans are unlikely to have considered any British tribe as a whole fit for privileged status, for everywhere the countrymen were by their standards backward.

Verulamium is not described in the ancient lists with a tribal name in the genitive following—though I have very little doubt that such tribal organization as survived was centred on it. Theoretically, therefore, the tribal capitals of any tribe for whom no town is designated in this way may have been similarly elevated; in fact most of these were difficult, small and poor, or otherwise backward, so that this is unlikely. The Trinovantes, however, are a different case. Their tribal capital at Colchester was, of course, taken for the site of the veteran settlement of the *Colonia Victricensis*. It may be that, when the colony was founded, the Trinovantes were given a new tribal capital in Caesaromagus at Widford,[25] but, as Professor Richmond has pointed out, there were many non-colonial residents at Colchester from the first and space was provided for them.[26] It is reasonable to suppose that the bulk of these residents were Trinovantes; and the survival of the *civitas Ubiorum* in the almost contemporary colony at Cologne would suggest that Claudius intended that the tribal institutions should survive at Colchester too, in a subordinate position to those of the colony.

There is one further point that the evidence allows us to consider. Where the tribal organization survived, were there any administrative units of a subsidiary type? I have already said that in the territory of the Helvetii after the promotion of the capital, there were a number of flourishing *vici*. Another useful piece of evidence comes from the territory of the Senones in northern France, where, as we learn from the career of a local notable,[27] in addition to the central tribal institutions, there were *pagi* in the rural areas, while the tribal capital of Agedincum was either itself a *vicus,* or divided into several *vici*. It is highly probable that Professor Frere is right to suggest that unchartered tribal capitals had, as minor built-up areas, the organization and the status of *vici,*[28] though there is in fact no unequivocal British evidence to confirm this. It may also be that in some or all of the tribes there were *pagi* or something like them, as sub-divisions of the rural areas; and the *curia Textoverdorum* which occurs at Chesterholm,[29] may well be such a rural sub-division. Unfortunately, the only attested British *vicus* is the one at Petuaria in the territory of the Parisi[30] and we have no information about the organization of this tribe—whether its tribal organization did survive, and if so whether the capital was at Petuaria or somewhere else.[31]

Obviously I have offered nothing here but a series of possibilities and guesses. Indeed I think it important to stress that the evidence does not support anything more. It looks probable that most Britons remained of peregrine status, with the tribe as the normal unit of local government, its institutions based on the tribal capital. Possibly, where this was so, the capital acquired the name of *vicus* and the appropriate organization for the handling of its specifically urban affairs, while other similarly organized groups may have developed within the tribal territory and more rural districts may have had a kind of *pagus*-organization. A few tribal capitals may have become chartered towns, though whether they achieved Latin or full Roman status we do not know (Latin is perhaps more probable); but in most cases it is likely that the country districts around them remained peregrine and retained a vestigial tribal organization, being *attributi* of their old tribal capital in its new chartered dignity. But there is almost nothing among these matters about which we can be certain. We need a great many more inscriptions to show which of the guesses are on or near the mark and which are not.[32]

NOTES

1 For an account of the municipal system see F. Abbott and A. C. Johnson, *Municipal Adminis-tration in the Roman Empire* (Princeton, 1926).

2 For some of the problems connected with Gallic towns see N. J. De Witt, *Urbanisation and the Franchise in Roman Gaul* (Lancaster, 1940). I accept Professor Frere's definition of *civitas* in this context, see *Antiquity*, xxxv (1961), 29 f.

3 Cf. *vergobret* in *C.I.L.*, xiii, 1048; the same man also held a post with the Latin title of *quaestor*. Later the chief magistrates here were probably called *IIviri* or *IIIIviri*, see *C.I.L.*, xiii, 1050.

4 For Aventicum see my article in *Revue Suisse de histoire*, 14 (1964) 387 f. I think that Aventicum was probably Latin, though many regard it as Roman in status; but the only point in my argument for this that is relevant here is that I can see no evidence that any new settlers were established there, i.e. the town seems to me to be a promoted native town.

5 *Civitas Lingonum*, *C.I.L.*, xiii, 5682, 5708; *colonia Lingonum*, *C.I.L.*, xiii, 5693.

6 *I.L.S.*, 6753.

7 Pomponius Mela, II.75 describing Narbonne as *Atacinorum Decimanorumque colonia*.

8 Tacitus, *Hist.*, IV.28 — *in Ubiis quod gens Germanicae originis eiurata patria Agrippinenses vocarentur;* and 65 — *deductis olim et nobiscum per conubium sociatis* ...

9 *C.I.L.*, vii, 11; there is of course also no evidence that monarchy did not survive, but for the tendency to oligarchy, see below.

10 *E.E.*, vii, 844.

11 *C.I.L.*, xvi, 49.

12 *C.I.L.*, vii, 863.

13 *C.I.L.*, vii, 775, 776.

14 *E.E.*, vii, 1052.

15 *J.R.S.*, xiv (1924), 244.

16 *E.E.*, ix, 1012.

17 *C.I.L.*, vii, 1165 = *E.E.*, ix, 635; but for a different reading, R. G. Collingwood *ap.* C. E. Stevens, *E.H.R.*, lii (1937), 201.

18 For a list, see A. L. F. Rivet, *Town and Country in Roman Britain* (London, 1958), 132.

19 See n.9.

20 *C.I.L.*, xii, 8771, 8773.

21 *C.I.L.*, xvi, 160; cf. Rivet, *loc. cit.*, p.65.

22 *E.E.*, ix, 985, cf. F. Haverfield, *Arch.*, lxi (1908), 215 f.

23 *E.E.*, ix, 986; the point was made and stressed by Professor Frere in discussion. Nevertheless I am not quite sure that this disposes of the value of the two texts, though I am not happy about the solution proposed by G. C. Boon in *Roman Silchester* (London, 1957), 76. A club of *peregrini* should mean a club of non-citizens, which implies, apparently, the existence of a citizenship of Calleva; it is obviously risky, however, to argue too strictly from the precise legal meaning of a word, which the Callevensians may not have known.

24 Tacitus, *Ann.*, xiv, 33; in discussion, Mr C. E. Stevens contested the validity of the argument from Tacitus, but is nevertheless prepared to accept the municipal status of Verulamium for other reasons.

25 As tentatively proposed by C. E. Stevens, *E.H.R.*, lii (1937), 198.

26 *Arch. J.*, ciii (1947), 31 f.

27 *C.I.L.*, xiii, 2949.

28 S. S. Frere, *Antiquity*, xxxv (1961), 31 f.

29 *E.E.*, ix, 593.

30 *J.R.S.*, xxviii (1938), 199.

31 But Professor Frere argues persuasively that it was, *loc. cit.*, 33 f.

32 In discussion, Mr C. E. Stevens took me to task, rightly, for failing to discuss a point often raised in connexion with my subject — that in France the chartered towns have regularly preserved their town-names into modern times (cf. Vienne from Vienna Allobrogum) while the unprivileged tribal capitals have preserved their tribal name (as Paris from Lutetia Parisiorum), so that the survival of town, not tribal names in Britain might suggest that British capitals were on the whole chartered. The facts are remarkable and interesting; but there are exceptions to the rule even in France (cf. Autun from Augustodunum, the tribal capital of the Aedui), and I do not feel that it provides a safe base for any conclusion.

INDUSTRY IN ROMAN BRITAIN
by
Professor Sir Ian Richmond

THE earliest clear example of an organized series of shops in a town of Roman Britain is that discovered by Professor S. S. Frere at Verulamium.[1] It comprises a block of shops in a row, fronted by a colonnade or portico, all built in timber and timber-framing, with wattle-and-daub plastered walls (Fig. 13). The shops are in part shops and in part workshops and there is no essential difference between the two. In this respect they resemble the small town shop of two generations ago, and of many generations before these, in which the stock of goods was not large and many purchases were the result of special orders, the goods being manufactured on the spot. Thus, the metal-workers[2] of the Verulamium shops operate their furnaces and smelting-pits in the front part of the premises open to public view, exactly as was seen in medieval towns and as may be seen in a Middle-Eastern town today. To realize this is to grasp what both shopping and industry most commonly meant in the classical world : for the mode is not confined to the provinces,[3] but is as true of Pompeii or Ostia as it is of Verulamium or, as will appear, of other Romano-British cantonal capitals or smaller towns.

At Wroxeter[4] very much the same conditions are repeated, with the difference that the buildings, while possibly set in a colonnade, are separate blocks, each comprising a long strip house or establishment with its narrow end on the valuable street frontage. These, again, are normally workshops and shops combined. But their planning, as at Verulamium and elsewhere, raises the question of living accommodation. If they were, as so many tombstones[5] show, family concerns or the concern of a slave or freedman (*libertus*) established there by a master or patron to run the business, where did the operators live? Sometimes, as is clear, they lived in rooms at the back of the shop;[6] but normally this space is hardly adequate for the purpose, and it is evident that in most cases they inhabited an upper storey above the shop, just as in the medieval world. Examples are to be seen on the reliefs of Trajan's Column[7] (Plate VIII) or on the occasional sarcophagus,[8] where the upper floor is often furnished with a balcony, as in actual examples[9] preserved in Rome, Ostia, and Pompeii. In medieval London[10] as illustrated in paintings of royal processions the same fashion is seen. The line of descent in Britain is not direct, as it was in the Mediterranean, but came back through Continental tradition and may thus be regarded as collateral. It lasted thenceforward until modern times, when it still survives in the old family business. It is the direct antithesis of the multiple store : not large-scale industry engaged in mass production of large stocks of standard goods, but a small concern producing to individual requirements goods specifically ordered, such as might be commissioned on one market-day and ready on the next.

PLATE VIII. Trajan's Column: shop with portico and upper storey on right.

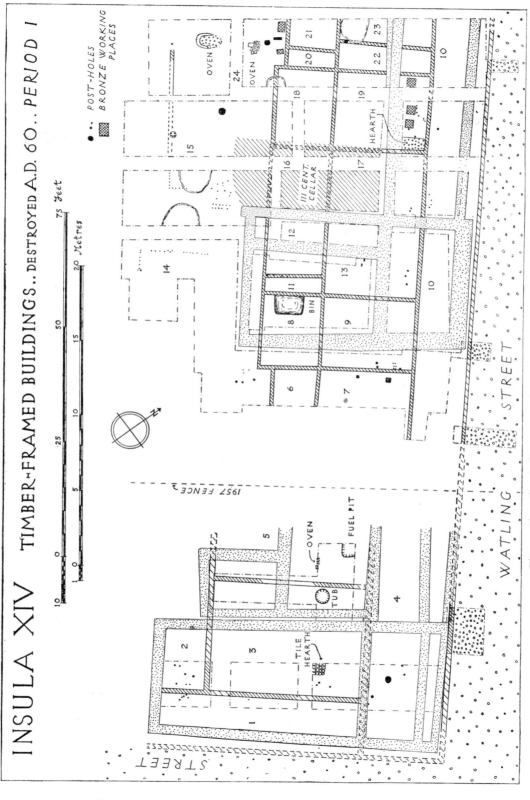

Fig. 13. Plan of early first-century shops in Insula XIV at Verulamium. (Reproduced by permission of the Society of Antiquaries and Professor S. S. Frere).

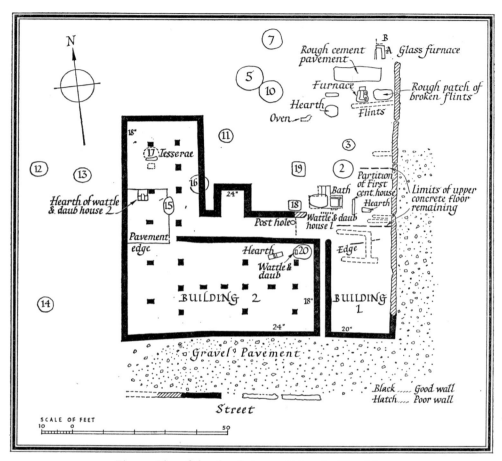

Fig. 14. Plan of the glass factory at Caistor-by-Norwich.
(*Reproduced by permission of the Society of Antiquaries*).

There were some shops which were larger establishments, more like a
house than a shop, as, for example, the glass manufactory[11] at Caistor St Edmund
(Venta Icenorum, Fig. 14). This was not a strip shop, and the glass-furnaces
which it contained were an integral part of the establishment and not a survival
from an earlier occupation. The limited number of the furnaces, as well as their
limited capacity, divorces them from mass production and puts them into the
category which is concerned with supplying a local market and local orders.
There is here no distinguishable difference between the cantonal capital and
the smaller tribal centres. Smaller places possessed exactly the same kind of
manufactories, as typified by the glass furnaces[12] of Wilderspool (Cheshire)
excavated by Thomas May. The origin of Wilderspool, with a Flavian occupation, must be regarded as military : later, however, the place certainly became

something like a *vicus,* and forms an excellent example of the abandoned fort-site[13] which kept some at least of its traders and here developed the silicaceous sand suited to glass-making. This type of development illustrates another important characteristic of ancient industry, namely, the tendency to exploit local resources for a local market when neither the resources nor the market itself were of large scale. Difficulties of transport here enter the picture and help to explain why such developments should be not only possible but, within the narrower ancient limits, profitable also.

The largest centres of population might indeed encourage larger enterprises, especially in food-production; for all must eat. It is significant that it should be Roman London[14] which produced, from Princes Street, the great donkey-mill for grinding corn. This is one of the few cases known in Britain of a bakery which was sufficiently large and important to demand animal power to drive its simple machinery. Others must have existed, but it is evident that such establishments were rare. The type is seen in detail at Pompeii and was taken for granted in Rome, but at Rome the city bakeries were worked by water-power, using the surplus flow (*aqua caduca*) from the city aqueducts. Procopius,[15] who makes the point, describes the inconvenience caused by the cutting of the aqueducts during the Gothic siege of A.D. 537 and the new arrangement, then invented, of placing the mills on rafts in the Tiber to be worked by the river current, a tradition which lasted into medieval and even more recent days.[16] This point would naturally raise the question how much use was made of water-power in Britain, where natural conditions favoured it so much more strongly than in the Mediterranean world. Meanwhile, however, it may be recollected that in Roman London there is widespread evidence in the form of small finds[17] for the working of bronze and copper in the same small-scale workshops as at Verulamium, as is indicated by the small size of the crucibles and ingots. This brings us back to the famous picture[18] of the Coronation procession of King Edward VI which is shown making its way along Cheapside. When the eye moves from the pageantry to its background it is struck by the shops lining the street, which are all long and narrow strip houses with upper floor or floors and shop-fronts shuttered and closed during the royal progress. But in essence the picture might also represent the shops of Roman London, in which the same type of family manufactory was conducted. Herein is illustrated the similarity of economic conditions and markets. Timber buildings might indeed turn into stone ones, as, for example, at Silchester,[19] where the main street is lined with such strip-shops. But in calling them shops it must again be emphasized that in at least two examples there is clear evidence for furnaces in the forepart of the building. In other words the customer could see honest work and craftsmanship in progress, or might even witness his order being executed. Workshop-establishments of this kind continued in use unchanged during Roman times and are attested at Silchester and Wroxeter, again to take examples only, down to the late-fourth or early-fifth centuries.

On the small scale thus to be envisaged complicated manufacturing processes might nevertheless take place, and may be revealed not by observation possible during excavation but by examination in the laboratory later. A striking example of such discovery is provided by the fragments of furnace linings submitted to Gowland from Silchester.[20] His own cursory impression was that they were ordinary oven linings or the like. Only analysis was to reveal the exceptionally interesting fact that they had been cupellation furnaces, used in the extraction of silver from lead or copper; and the fact was disclosed by the large deposit of bone-ash which was still mixed with the drops at the bottom of the furnace. From the base of the furnace thus identified Gowland reconstructed[21] the whole apparatus, basing his reconstruction upon the simple furnaces of workshops illustrated in a Japanese drawing. The result is a small furnace with a clay dome or cover renewed on each occasion of operation, the artificial blast from bellows being applied through the top (Fig. 15). The building in which the furnace was found looks at first sight like a small courtyard house, in which case the furnace, of which the base is recorded, lay in the court. That arrangement, however, is inherently unlikely, since it would imply that the furnace, in which was developed a very high temperature, might frequently be exposed to rain. The likelihood, then, is that the space was roofed. The building also had hypocausts, but it is uncertain whether these were contemporary with the furnace. Whether this was so or not, the establishment plainly ranks as a little factory rather than the normal shop, for its plan has nothing to do with a strip house (Fig. 16).

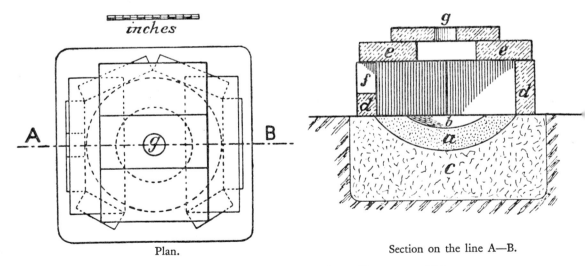

Plan.   Section on the line A—B.

Fig. 15. A cupellation furnace in Insula X, House 4, at Silchester.
(Reproduced by permission of the Society of Antiquaries).

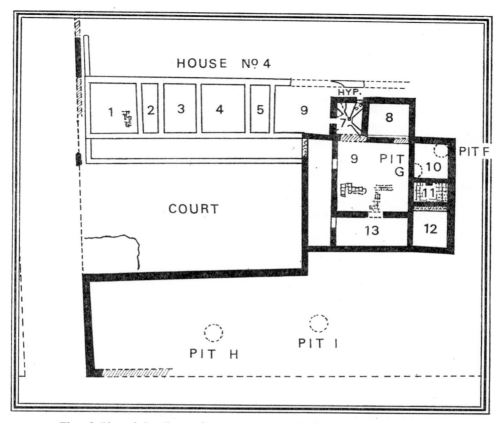

Fig. 16. Plan of the silver refinery workshop at Silchester (Insula X, House 4).
(*Reproduced by permission of the Society of Antiquaries*).

There were other manufacturing establishments at Silchester,[22] though the excavators were often in doubt as to their purpose, and these doubts cannot but be shared by anyone who studies the original account. For example, the concern which is described as dye-works[23] offers the bases of structures which are like supports for great vats or coppers. They are, indeed, manifestly quite different from the bases of such structures as bread-ovens. But no proof that they were dyeing vats was obtained, because the bases were high and ploughing had sheared off their tops. On the other hand, they are too numerous to belong to a cook-shop, nor are they accompanied by the complement of tanks to be associated with a fullery. These suggestions dismissed, that of coppers for dyeing still remains the most acceptable, though in default of material susceptible of analysis it must remain a working hypothesis only.

Here a return may be made to the point that, in relation to workshops and small-scale maunfacture, small country centres are no less important than the larger towns, because of the localization and individualization of industry. This is illustrated by an air-photograph,[24] taken by Dr St Joseph, of Alchester (Oxon.), which shows the main street lined by strip shops, distinguishable now by their walls and now by their stone floors. The importance of the record is that it shows a *vicus* or *pagus*-centre—the exact status of the place is as yet unknown—serving as a local market centre. The state of affairs is reminiscent of the smaller towns of nineteenth-century Oxfordshire, before the coming of the internal combustion engine made possible the concentration of traffic in the principal centre of Oxford itself. Today Oxford is a busier market-town than ever in its existence and round it the little towns decay. But in the era of horse-drawn traffic or pedestrian journeys—nobody now thinks of walking seven miles there and seven miles back to market—the little towns flourished and this is one of the reasons why there were so many small towns in Roman Britain, as has been so much more fully realized in the last fifteen years. It was just such a small centre, the little town of Great Chesterford in Essex, which yielded the magnificent group of iron-work[25] now exhibited in the Cambridge University Museum of Archaeology and Ethnology. Unlike many other hoards of iron objects, this one comprises the objects which a local iron-smith was making rather than his tools. Among the household articles one of the most magnificent is a cauldron or pot-hanger chain, richly wrought, with swivels and links of gay complexity yet sound utilitarian purpose. It is matched only by the equally fine example now in the Corinium Museum at Cirencester. Among the tools one of the most remarkable is a fine pair of cropping shears, used in cloth manufacture for trimming the nap, as one of the final processes of making good woollen cloth. Records of the Yorkshire cloth industry indicate how such cloth was spun and woven in the home and brought into town for processing and finishing in the little workshops. There the cropping shears were used in conjunction with an ammoniac liquid kept in a great vessel, in exactly the same way as the urine[26] collected for this purpose in Roman towns. Here classical literature and the household stage in the development of classical industry meet, and remind us also of the mosaics of North Africa, depicting the spinning shepherdesses.[27] Such women are not romantic figures in Dresden or Meissen china: their spare time in the fields is occupied in picking and spinning the wool left by their flocks on bushes or any object that would catch it, and they would be expected to return at the end of the day with so much thread to their credit. The cropping shears are thus a link between town and countryside or rural and urban economy, an implement which unites the villa economy with the town and manufactory. Another interesting problem is posed by the enormous scythes, far larger than any wielded today, even by the most powerful man. The question of physique is here important, since Romano-British skeletal remains do not normally run to figures of great stature. Are these scythes, then, the fittings for a reaping-machine which was an improvement upon the kind figured on the sepulchral monument[28] of Buzenol? For machinery of another type was certainly one of the products of this manufactory. The objects include the iron shaft, or spindle, which was the vertical member in a water-mill, the shaft being provided with three stout blade-like wings which are fitted into the stone in order to grip it for rotation. A similar example is known from Great Chesterford,[29] and the mechanism is described by Vitruvius[30] as applied to water-mills. This raises again the question of the use of water-power mentioned above. The stone hub-core of a substantial water-wheel,[31] working in a horizontal plane and related to a mill-race still visible, is known from the North Tyne bridge at the Roman fort of Chesters: but two others like it were found in fragmentary state in the River Witham, just outside the south wall of the enlarged *colonia* at Lincoln[32] (Plate IX). These must have been connected with industrial activity, flour-milling being one possibility, saw-milling another; for, like flour-milling, saw-milling by water-power is mentioned in antiquity, if only in passing, by Ausonius[33] in his poem on the River Moselle. Its tributary, the Ruwer, was harnessed to noisy water-mills engaged in sawing stone.

These links with the mechanical side of industry, whose modest developments never got so far as to induce a Roman industrial revolution, recall other manufactured products of Romano-British towns. The jet industry[34] of York is worth attention. This remarkable material, obtained in commercial quantity from the Whitby lias in Yorkshire, had properties of magnetic attraction and curious qualities in relation to oil and water which made the Roman world[35] regard it as magical. Quite apart from this it had qualities of beauty. It was therefore attractive as a medium for jewellery and small ornamental objects, for which the great vogue in Victorian days reminds us that the material appealed to other ages than the Roman. Many simple utilitarian objects like hair-pins and distaffs were therefore made of jet in Roman York, where wasters and cores from their manufacture have been found. But the elaborate articles are more fascinating. The Gorgon-headed amulets,[36] to ward off the evil eye, or the port-rait medallions[37] of family groups, or the very complicated articulated bangles and necklaces are of a richness only rivalled in the second great centre of Roman jet products, namely, Cologne. This raises an interesting point. While it is quite certain from the manufacturers' waste that jet was worked in York, no waste of the kind has yet appeared in Cologne. In any case the raw material must have come to the Rhineland from Britain, since it occurs in quantity, as at Whitby, nowhere else in Europe. Yet if jet had been manufactured at Cologne, as were enamel and glass objects,[38] would it not have been distributed, as these products were, in the trade with the free German outlands east of the Rhine which blossomed so freely in the third and fourth centuries? But if the jet objects were imported from Britain to Cologne as manufactured goods which were highly prized and not for re-export, their absence in Free Germany would be understandable.

Humbler though much more productive industries are seen at the *colonia* of Colchester, where potteries and their kilns surround the town and almost encircle it.[39] This emphasizes the point that in Roman chartered towns local law[40] might prohibit the presence inside the town of tile kilns which had more than the most limited capacity. It also suggests that in many cases the heavier or dirtier industries are not to be sought inside the town at all but on its outskirts; and this should give pause to those who study a town-plan and remark upon the paucity of industry without information of what may, or may not, have been established outside the walls. At Colchester the most interesting group of kilns is concerned with the manufacture of samian ware.[41] The kilns are complicated and the ware is plentiful, though it impresses rather by its quantity of output than its quality of decoration. Yet the decoration[42] has specific characteristics of style. It is crowded and vivid, intended for a public much interested in beast-shows and gladiatorial combats, in other words with the amphitheatre; and the scenes include an interest, positively eighteenth-century in flavour, in the execution of criminals. But barbotine wares were also made in the Colchester kilns and these are of the highest interest, for they reflect the beliefs of the countryside. Stag-headed men[43] are here, with wild stag-horn head-dresses. This belongs to the world out of which the scenes in *The Merry Wives of Windsor* grew, when joking had removed the seriousness of belief. Dwarfs[44] appear, and elves such as might come fresh from a fairy-tale. Other scenes are less easy to interpret, though the phallic decoration[45] plainly derives from the classical world. The work in general, however, belongs to a native tradition rich in fantasy and eloquent of the countryside which it was serving. As for the marketing of the wares, and of pottery in general, Colchester[46] has yielded pottery stores or shops in the heart of the town. But Wroxeter indicates a simpler method of trade. The fire which wrecked the Forum in the later second century caused the collapse into the gutter of the colonnade of masses of objects on sale in temporary stalls,[47] reminiscent of those still erected in market-places and set up for market-day only. The piles of pottery or whetstones exactly resemble those brought to market today in Spain or Africa by pack-horses with panniers, the stock often consisting of one pack-horse load only, and even glove manufacturers might sell their wares in this way.

Two more examples of trades based upon much rarer evidence may close the picture. York Museum is famous for its remarkable sarcophagus burials in which the corpse in its winding-sheet and with its accompanying objects were enveloped in liquid gypsum that has set hard and retains their detailed impressions when well preserved. The cloth impressions[48] indicate much use of linen. This implies a flax industry, which in turn demands abundant water for the soaking of the plant to separate its fibres. In the York district it is the valley of the lower Ouse and the fens of Holderness which would best furnish such

PLATE IX. Fragment of stone hub of a mill-wheel from Lincoln.
(*By courtesy of the City and County Museum, Lincoln*).

PLATE X. Stone mould for pewter vessel from Lansdown, Bath (cf. Fig. 17).

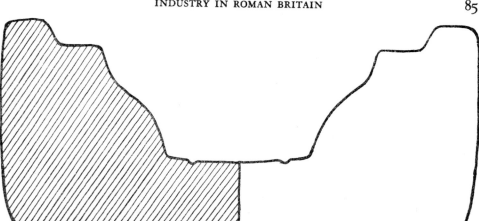

Fig. 17 Section of stone mould for pewter vessel from Lansdown, Bath (cf. Plate X).

conditions: indeed it must be recognized that this is the sole tract of country in Yorkshire really suited to the growing and treatment of flax. The gypsum impressions related to local physical geography thus supply the evidence for a special trade and its location. The second example of an equally striking kind comes from Bath, where are stored the finds from a headland site in the Lansdown area some seven miles north of the town and about half a mile east of the Fosse Way. These comprise forms or moulds for making pewter dishes, carved in an exceptionally fine lias stone.[49] The headland promontory is not itself the source of the stone but the site for the furnaces, a high point which would ensure a draught that every wind would bring. The moulds themselves comprise forms for the dishes, plates or trays, in various shapes from plain to decorated, and also for ornamental features such as handles, medallions, and the like, which were to be made separately and brazed on to the vessel (Plate X; Fig. 17). This manufactory, situated in the heart of the country, is a culminating example of local enterprise, though how it was related to local society is less certain. In the broadest sense, it must be concerned with the different ways in which the great tribal land-owners, the *decuriones,* developed their property. But such development was also conditioned by the individual interest in small-scale manufacture and the small-scale exploitation of natural resources and the possibilities of local profits. It was an era in which industry as understood today scarcely existed, and when home industries were much more the regular way of development; when the trader was often half-shopkeeper and half-manufacturer, and when the small-scale manufacturer would take his own wares to market, as Heywood Sumner[50] first taught us of the New Forest potters. Organizations of larger scale certainly existed for commodities in bulk, especially in relation to imports from overseas, where ships' cargoes are in question. But the final emphasis must be upon the small scale, in a world of individualists.

NOTES

1 S. S. Frere, *Antiq. J.*, xxxix (1959), 3-4, fig. 2.
2 *Ibid.*, 4.
3 For shop-workshops at Pompeii, see A. Mau and F. W. Kelsey, *Pompeii, its life and art* (1899), 270-272; at Ostia, R. Meiggs, *Roman Ostia* (1960), 271-274.
4 Wroxeter, J. P. Bushe-Fox, *Excavations on the site of the Roman town at Wroxeter in 1912* (*Antiquaries Research Report*, I, 1913), 22, fig. 8.
5 For example, G. Calza, *Ostia, Necropoli*, 252, fig. 150, pl. xxvii *a*.
6 *Wroxeter*, J. P. Bushe-Fox, *loc. cit.*
7 Trajan's Column, C. Cichorius, *Die Reliefs der Traianssäule*, Taf. 6, 26, 63, 65, 73.
8 Déchelette, *Manuel d'Archéologie*, vi, 2, 202, fig. 68, from Lateran Museum, l'arrivée au relais.
9 Balconies, Rome, E. Nash, *Pictorial Dictionary of Ancient Rome*, I, 506, fig. 603. Ostia, R. Meiggs, *Roman Ostia* (1960), pl. viii *b*. Pompeii, A. Maiuri, *Pompeii* (1955), pl. xxxix.
10 London painting, Sir W. H. St John Hope, *Cowdray and Eastbourne Park* (1919), 54, pl. xvi.
11 Caistor St Edmund, D. Atkinson, *Caister Excavations* (1931), pl. xii.
12 Wilderspool, T. May, *Warrington's Roman Remains* (1904), 40-58.
13 G. Webster. in this volume, see p. 32.
14 E. B. Birley, *Antiq. J.*, ix (1929), 221, fig. 1.
15 *De Bell. Got.*, i, 19.
16 For the medieval and later mills, see Egger, *Römischer Veduten*, i, 64; and S. B. Platner and T. Ashby, *A topographical dictionary of Ancient Rome* (1929), 350, pl. 35.
17 R. E. M. Wheeler, *London in Roman times* (1930), 32, pl. vii, A.
18 See note 10.
19 Silchester, J. Ward, *Romano-British Buildings and Earthworks* (1911), 183, fig. 56.
20 *Arch.*, lvii (1900), 113.
21 *Ibid.* 118-119, figs. 2, 3.
22 *Arch.*, liv (1895), 450, pl. xlvi, Insula XII, blocks III and IV, Insula X, block IV.
23 *Arch.*, liv (1895), 460.
24 J. K. St Joseph, *J.R.S.*, xliii (1953), 92.
25 Cambridge CHESTERFORD IRON. *Arch. J.*, xiii (1856), 1, pls. 1-3.
26 Macrobius, *Sat.*, iii, 16, 15.
27 M. Rostovtzeff *Social and Economic History of the Roman Empire* (1926), 290, pl. xlvii, 3.
28 J. Mertens, *Archaeologia Belgica*, 42, 83, pl. xv.
29 Great Chesterford water-mill shaft, *Arch. J.*, xiii, pl. 3, n. 28.
30 Vitruvius, *de Architectura*, x, 10, 2.
31 Collingwood Bruce, *Handbook to the Roman Wall* (11th edn. 1957), 85.
32 Not yet published.
33 *Mosella* 362-4, (Erubris) praecipiti torquens cerealia saxa rotatu, stridentesque trahens per levia marmora serras, audit perpetuos ripa ex utraque tumultus.
34 R.C.H.M., *Eburacum, Roman York* (1962), 141.
35 *Ibid.*, 141-2, quoting Pliny, *Nat. Hist.*, xxxvi, 141 and Solinus *Coll. rer. mem.*, 22, 11.
36 R.C.H.M., *op. cit.*, pl. 68, nos. H. 230·1, H. 321·14, H. 2443 (the finest).
37 *Ibid.*, nos. H. 2442 and H. 2444.
38 H. J. Eggers, *Der Römische Import in Freien Germanien*, Tafeln 14-16, Karten 4-5, etc.
39 M. R. Hull, *The Roman potters' kilns at Colchester* (*Soc. Antiq. Research Report*, xxi) 1963, 1, fig. 1.
40 C. G. Bruns, *Fontes Iuris Romani antiqui*, part I (Ed. 7, 1909), 128, Lex Ursonensis, lxxvi: figlinas teglarias maiores tegularum CCC tegulariumq. in oppido colon. Iul. ne quis habeto.
41 M. R. Hull, *op. cit.*, 20-34, 43-90.
42 M. R. Hull, *op. cit.*, 51-68, figs. 20-37 *passim*; cf. 94, fig. 51 in barbotine.
43 M. R. Hull, *op. cit.*, 96, fig. 53, 13.
44 *Ibid.*, fig. 53, 8.
45 *Ibid.*, fig. 53, 1, fig. 54, 2.
46 *Roman Colchester*, 153, 198.
47 D. Atkinson, *Report on the Excavations at Wroxeter 1923-27* (1942), 127-9, pl. 31.
48 R.C.H.M., *Eburacum, Roman York*, 95, pl. 33, 108-9.
49 P.S.A.L.,², xxii (1907-9), 34-38; cf. W. J. Wedlake, *Excavations at Camerton, Somerset 1926-56*, 81-86, fig. 27, pl. xvii, where the previous reference is incorrectly given.
50 Heywood Sumner, *Excavations in the New Forest Roman pottery sites* (1927), 53-54.

THE END OF TOWNS IN ROMAN BRITAIN

by

Professor S. S. Frere

THE way in which the towns of Roman Britain came to an end, and the date at which this happened, has always been a problem which has exercised the fancy of historians. Gildas, who was the nearest in time to the period in question, has a purple passage in which he compares the Saxon sack of cities with the work of the Assyrians of old, and describes in vivid terms the slaugher, the unburied corpses, and the burning and overthrow of buildings.[1] In the absence of other kinds of evidence, this sort of picture seemed suitable enough in a land where Saxon conquerors were thought of as driving out and replacing the earlier inhabitants and their whole civilization. And early excavators, as at Wroxeter[2] in 1860, when they found "everywhere in and near the baths and basilica abundant ashes as of a conflagration and many skeletons, some in the streets and five even in the hypocausts . . ." naturally drew the conclusion that Gildas was right.

It is only slowly that evidence of various kinds has accumulated, largely from new excavation, but also from a study of Saxon sources, to redress the picture of universal slaughter. In the first place we have the undoubted fact that while a few towns in Roman Britain such as Verulamium, Wroxeter, Caistor-by-Norwich, or Kenchester are now empty sites, and were clearly deserted either after sack or for some other reason, the majority of the important town sites like London, Winchester, Canterbury, York, Exeter, Cirencester, or Lincoln are still occupied. They might have been re-occupied after a period of emptiness because of the inevitability of the choice of the original site, and the compulsion of communications or other economic factors, but it is perhaps more likely that they never ceased to be occupied: and this has been proved at some. Secondly, the excavators of Silchester found no signs of burning or slaughter or sack, but came to the conclusion that the town was abandoned[3] after slow decay. The idea of evacuations of towns had some warrant from the Anglo-Saxon Chronicle, and it was widely believed that as the tide of Saxon conquest advanced the Britons had to retire before it, until the moment was reached when they were almost all crowded into Wales and the Dumnonian peninsula, from which they overflowed to Brittany.

The key word in this picture is Saxon *conquest*. But in more recent years it has come to be realized that this picture of organized conquest, leading to refugees streaming back before the advance, as they did in 1940, is not an accurate description of what happened. In the first place, of course, even by A.D. 600 there were large parts of Britain outside Wales and Dumnonia still held by Britons : but these were not areas in which there had been many towns. The lowland zone, which was the area where the urban civilization of Roman Britain had flourished, *had* by then been over-run.

Secondly we can see that the Saxon settlement of the lowland zone was the result of a long and complicated history, starting with the official settlement of Germanic mercenary soldiers on land in Britain as *laeti* or *foederati* by imperial or provincial officials themselves, for the purpose of defending the province against northern aggression by Picts and against further encroachment by Saxons. About or soon after 450 there was a rebellion of these mercenaries against British authority—there may have been other rebellions earlier—and for a time there was warfare. But at the battle of Mount Badon, perhaps in 486,[4] the tide was turned, and a period of British prosperity set in, which lasted until about 550. Clearly, if a town could survive in some fashion until Mount Badon, it could continue thereafter in prosperity until 550, as far as the Saxons were concerned.

Thirdly, it is becoming clear that the whole conception implicit in the words Saxon conquest is misleading. There were one or two battles or sieges, and the tide of armies fluctuated. But the real process of Saxon settlement was a slow, gradual, penetration into areas of countryside where the breakdown of the Romano-British economic system had left a solitude.

That is the Saxon side of it. On the British side we have (i) the recently established fact that around 369 many, if not all, of the town-walls of Roman Britain were modernized by the addition of ballista-towers and the strengthening of their ditch systems. This must have immensely increased their capacity to hold out long into the fifth century, especially when we remind ourselves of the point so well put by Professor E. A. Thompson[5] about the almost total incapacity of Germanic armies to capture a fortified town if it was defended. They lacked siege-engines, and they lacked defensive armour : even their spears and swords were of little use, and they were "at a disastrous disadvantage when assailing the walls of a Roman town". Furthermore the highly-organized commissariat branch of the Roman army was a thing unknown in barbarian circles. Each man had to supply his own food. The Romans could counter a barbarian invasion by driving all the livestock, and transporting the grain, within the walls of towns, and by leaving the invaders to starve and scatter, almost as effectively as by meeting them in the field. This, it is worth suggesting, is one of the purposes of the multitude of walled towns, some no larger than walled villages, that is one of the features of the western provinces in the later Roman period. It was a passive defence in depth, a series of hedgehogs, and, provided the country-dwellers could be made to react in time, it could be a very effective defence : provided finally that the walled towns themselves were willing and equipped to hold out. (ii) There is the even more recent demonstration by Mrs Sonia Hawkes of the presence of items of uniform belonging to late Germanic auxiliary forces in many of our towns.[6] Her first map is of metal-work thought to be of continental origin and to date from 369 onwards. There is a large group from Richborough and one find from Bradwell; there are one certain military burial from Dorchester-on-Thames and two probable others from elsewhere; and the remainder come from towns—London, Leicester, Caistor-by-Norwich, and Catterick. If these items represent the equipment of continental forces brought over in 369, there are obvious gaps both on the Saxon Shore and also in the north. The second map is of buckles, etc., made in Britain, but designed for military uniforms of the same sort of troops. They begin soon after 369, but may go down well into the fifth century. Apart from Richborough, they seem to concentrate mainly in the towns of Roman Britain, and they suggest the possible steps taken by the *civitates* of Britain to defend themselves after Honorius' rescript of 410. Again there are gaps in the distribution which, now that this class has been recognized, further work will surely fill.

It is interesting to compare these maps with O'Neil's well-known map of Theodosian coin-hoards.[7] Except from Catterick and Stanwick there are no buckle finds north of the Humber; but leaving aside the Coastal Signal Stations, we would certainly expect future discoveries at York itself and at some of the late inland forts. Apart from this, however, the area compares well with that in which we have the coin evidence for continued Roman control in the latest period. To supplement the picture provided by the equipment and the coin hoards, we have the suggestion recently made by Mr Kenneth Painter[8] that the silver ingots in the shape of the double axe which appear in Britain in the late fourth century were used for paying troops. The distribution of these is south-eastern, at Richborough, Canterbury, London, and Stanmore: and some fragments also in the Coleraine hoard.

When we come to the towns themselves we can therefore now arrive fortified with the knowledge that at the end of the fourth century their defences had been brought up to date; that they seem to have contained Germanic troops to man these defences; and that the Saxon settlers would be ill-equipped to take them by force. On the other hand the Germanic garrisons themselves might be a potential danger, since at least in Kent we know they eventually revolted.

In considering the towns, it is as well to distinguish between those in the east of Britain and those further west. Those in the east lay in areas which were soon taken over by Saxon settlers, while those further west remained free for longer. In both cases, of course, the breakdown of the Romano-British economic system will have brought disastrous results to town life, but further west the towns may have struggled on longer in being. The collapse of money circulation, according to Dr J. P. C. Kent,[9] was complete by 430, but this may not in itself have been disastrous, for it is doubtful how much reliance can have been placed on the coinage, or how deeply its use penetrated, from quite early in the fourth century. There had been serious inflation on a growing scale throughout the century, and towards the end of it the supply of coin was seriously interrupted: in the circumstances barter will already have played an important part in every-day life. More serious for the towns was the decay of trade and industry. Indeed,

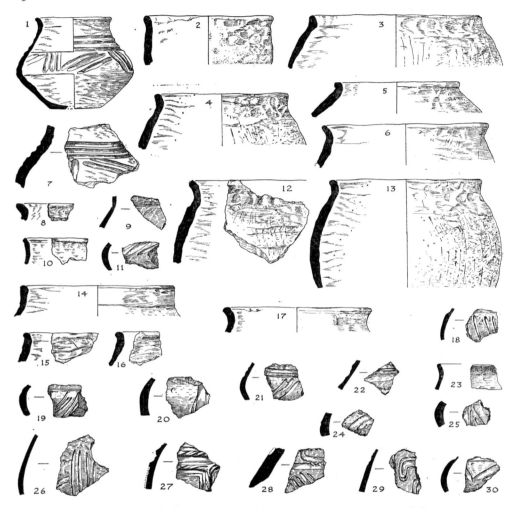

Fig. 18. Fifth-century Anglo-Frisian pottery from Canterbury (¼)

1.   Hard grey sandy ware with fine shell-grit, some dissolved out; surface unevenly burnished with narrow strokes mainly horizontal; decoration in shallow grooves.
2.   Hard grey finely granulated ware, uneven surface; burnished on rim and patchily on body, which remains gritty.
3.   Hard grey sandy ware.
4,6.   Ware as 1.
5.   Grey sandy ware, surface and lip smoothly burnished.
7,9.   Smooth grey ware.
8,10.   Finely granulated grey ware, uneven smoothly burnished surfaces.
12.   Hard finely granulated light grey ware, gritty where burnishing is worn or absent: outside roughly trimmed, and finger-marks on neck.
13.   Ware as 1. Partly burnished outside; rather rough vertical trimming.
14.   Ware as 2.
15.   Light grey-buff ware, with fine shell-grit.
16,17.   Ware as 1.
11,18-30. Sherds of Anglo-Frisian pottery: smooth fine grey ware, decoration in shallow grooves or (no. 27) raised twisted cables.

one of the serious obstacles to fifth-century archaeology is the fact that at some point in it, before late fourth-century fashions had changed, pottery was no longer produced, once the factories, in which production had been centralized in the later fourth century, went out of business. More serious still will have been the growing insecurity of the countryside, for Romano-British towns were to a great extent parasitic on the countryside, and the breakdown of food supply would lead to desertion. There is evidence for threatened breakdown at Verulamium.

Venta Icenorum is one of the towns where military equipment, and the presence of two important early Germanic cemeteries outside the walls, suggest that the place was garrisoned in the way I have described. Excavations there in 1930 found the remains of at least 36 people in a large house which had been burnt down about A.D. 400. This suggests a rebellion of the garrison if not a sack by hostile forces, and is an event in the Gildas tradition. On the other hand, it is only one building in the town, and we have no information that others were burnt down, and must beware of generalization from insufficient evidence.[10] The cemeteries outside the walls of Caistor contain objects which can be dated to 390-400.[11] At first the mercenaries no doubt served the purpose for which they were placed there, but there is every reason to suppose that their rebellion took place fairly early in the fifth century, in the 420s or 430s if not before.

Canterbury is another Romano-British city lying in an area where we know there were early settlements of Germanic mercenaries. From the late fourth century, perhaps from 360 onwards, a rather primitive-looking hand-made pottery was becoming increasingly common. Some of it has a distinctly Belgic appearance. I do not know where it was made, but examples have been found also at Lullingstone villa. This is the latest Romano-British pottery at Canterbury, and it may have continued into the fifth century. I used to think it was purely fifth-century, but now know that it certainly started earlier. But we also have some early Germanic pottery, though so far no military equipment.

The Germanic pottery is Anglo-Frisian (Fig.18), and the earliest sherds may date, on continental analogies, to c. A.D. 400. Several sherds have been found singly, but there is one Insula where there seems to have been an orderly settlement (Fig. 19). Just behind the old Marlowe Theatre, excavations in advance of the enlargement of the Theatre cut along what I now realize was the edge of a hut; it was overlying the remains of an earlier Roman timber-framed building, but by the early fifth century, if not before, this house had disappeared and the site was vacant. In 1960 there was an opportunity for excavation at the other end of the Insula, below the playground of the old Simon Langton School. This excavation was carried out by Mr J. S. Wacher to begin with, and later by Miss M. G. Wilson. Here parts of six huts were found strung out in a line parallel with the Roman street and about 30 ft from it (Fig. 20). They were all the sunken type of hut, consisting of a floor cut into the soil to a depth of about 1-2 ft. It is often thought that such huts accompany larger surface-built halls in the capacity of

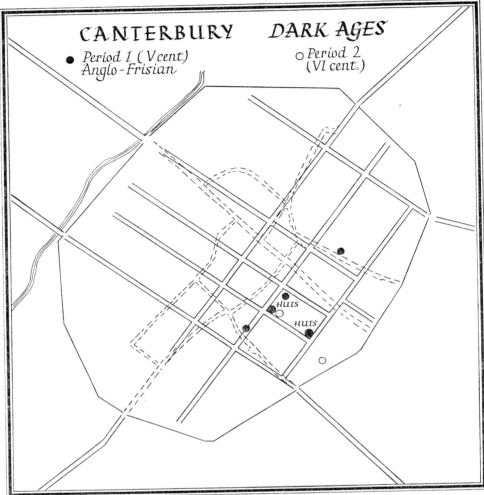

Fig. 19. The distribution of early post-Roman pottery in the Canterbury excavations.

weaving- or cooking-huts : but there is quite good evidence that in Britain they
sometimes, if not always, formed the only kind of building in Anglo-Saxon
villages, as Professor E. M. Jope's excavations at Cassington[12] have shown. In
Canterbury, owing to the disturbance of the soil caused by medieval and later pits
and foundations, we cannot be sure that no larger halls existed contempor-
aneously : but there is no evidence for them. The row of huts is suggestive in
itself that the type was self-sufficing, and at any rate at this early date we may
accept that they formed the abodes of settlers or mercenaries of the rank and file.

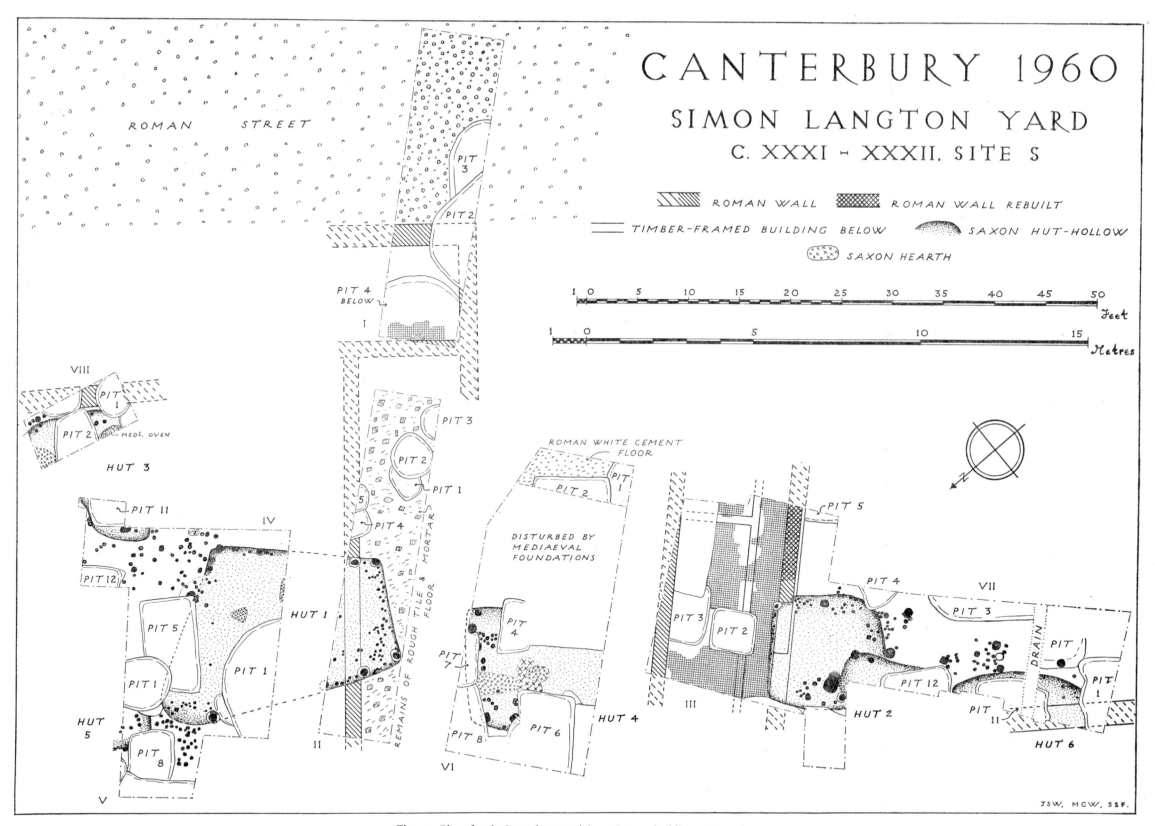

CANTERBURY 1960
SIMON LANGTON YARD
C. XXXI - XXXII, SITE S

ROMAN STREET

ROMAN WALL   ROMAN WALL REBUILT

TIMBER-FRAMED BUILDING BELOW   SAXON HUT-HOLLOW

SAXON HEARTH

PIT 3

PIT 2

PIT 4 BELOW

I

VIII

PIT 1

PIT 2   MEDL. OVEN

HUT 3

PIT 3

PIT 2

PIT 1

5

PIT 4

ROMAN WHITE CEMENT FLOOR

PIT 2   PIT 1

PIT 11

IV

DISTURBED BY MEDIAEVAL FOUNDATIONS

PIT 5

PIT 3   PIT 2

PIT 4   VII

PIT 12

PIT 5

HUT 1

REMAINS OF ROUGH TILE & MORTAR FLOOR

PIT 4

PIT 3

DRAIN   PIT 1

PIT 5

PIT 1

PIT 4

PIT 7

PIT 12

PIT 1

HUT 5

PIT 1

II

PIT 8   PIT 6

III

HUT 2

PIT 11

HUT 6

PIT 8

VI

HUT 4

V

JSW, MGW, SSF.

Fig. 20. Plan of early Saxon huts overlying a Roman building at Canterbury.

It is possible that the Simon Langton huts are slightly later in date than the Marlowe Theatre one, but they should still belong to the middle or second half of the fifth century. Starting with this fifth-century pottery, the Saxon series at Canterbury seems to be, as far as I can tell, continuous. Sixth-century pottery comes from a later hut near the Marlowe Theatre and thereafter follow the straw-tempered wares. The town was never deserted; occupation of a sort was continuous, but by degrees civic discipline will have broken down. Pits were dug in streets, and the streets themselves will have become encumbered by the ruins of Roman buildings. In this way the street of medieval Canterbury, when it emerged, bore little relation to the Roman except at the gates. A feature of many sites in Canterbury is a thick layer of rather fine-grained black soil which contains large quantities of late Roman pottery, but which intervenes stratigraphically between the late Roman and the medieval layers or the Saxon when they are present. I understand that similar layers have been noticed at Winchester, Chichester and Cirencester. It is difficult to explain them except perhaps as the accumulation of wind-blown dust, household rubbish, decayed thatch, and disintegrating timber buildings, which is likely to accumulate when civic discipline has disappeared. Soon after the middle of the fifth century Canterbury had become a Saxon or Anglo-Frisian town; and this accords with the Anglo-Saxon chronicle, which under 455 records that Hengist rebelled against Vortigern and took the kingdom: and under 457 "Hengist fought the Britons at a place called Crecganford and slew four thousand men, and the Britons left Kent and fled to London in great terror." The wealth of the Roman town, as it neared its end, is illustrated by the recently discovered hoard of silver which had been concealed just outside the London gate. There were 8 coins ending with Honorius and Arcadius, 11 silver spoons, 2 silver ingots, 1 silver pin, 1 silver implement, and a gold ring, and a gold hook and eye.

A somewhat similar picture is presented by my recent excavations at Dorchester-on-Thames, and there also a small late silver hoard is known. Just outside Dorchester the well-known Germanic burials in the Dyke Hills and elsewhere produced military equipment which Mrs Sonia Hawkes has recently re-studied: its date is late fourth-century and its context lies in the Roman auxiliary forces of *laeti*. Dorchester, of course, is not a cantonal capital, and strictly speaking I ought not to mention it at this conference; but evidence for my period is so hard to find that to do so briefly can hardly be avoided.

Dorchester is one of a small group of sites in Britain where the coinage of the Theodosian period, instead of dwindling to 1 or 2% of the total, actually rises considerably. This state of affairs is very rare and must mean that official payments, or at any rate provision of small change, were maintained here to a much greater extent than elsewhere. We can hardly avoid associating this with the mercenaries, though exactly why it should be so here and not in Canterbury or Caistor remains obscure. My excavations have taken place amongst the cabbages of the allotments in the south-west corner of the small walled enclosure. Beside the street which forms the axis of the town stood a small building of three rooms, which overlay a coin of Honorius, but which was cut by Saxon disturbances. All that survives are the unmortared stone footings, and they are so slight as to suggest a half-timbered upper structure. In 1963, excavations a little further north revealed scanty traces of further similar buildings, but in this case so thoroughly robbed that the plan was not recoverable. These stone footings were the only stone structures found anywhere in the excavations; earlier buildings had been entirely timber-framed. Thus they represent an innovation on the site, and might well be considered as the simple housing provided for the military force in garrison. Further north still there was excavated a Saxon hut of the type with sunken floor. Its doorway was entered down 3 steps from the Roman street; but its date is somewhat later than the Canterbury huts, being assignable on pottery evidence to the middle of the sixth century or perhaps a few years earlier. Here again therefore we have a town taken over by Saxon settlers or soldiers, and occupation is continuous from Roman times : there are a few pieces of Anglo-Frisian pottery to show early or mid-fifth-century occupation, though no huts of this period have yet appeared.

Excavations at Cirencester have not yet, as far as I know, thrown much light on the end of the Roman town. The Forum had been adequately maintained and cleaned well into the fifth century, and the absence of coins on the extremely worn flagging of its piazza suggests that it survived until after 430. Elsewhere in the town streets continued to be resurfaced, and the silt from the worn limestone metalling continued to invade, and eventually engulf, the colonnades of buildings. Finally came a time when no silt invaded a newly cut street-ditch[13] which suggests that wheeled traffic was dwindling to vanishing-point; and in this ditch some human skeletons were found. It is difficult to see how even in a very decayed town bodies could be left to rot on the edges of streets, and Mr Wacher has suggested to me that they may be a result of the great plague of 443 or the following years which is attested by Gildas and Hydatius.[14] Pestilence might easily have an unexpectedly disastrous influence on the fortunes of a fifth-century city, no less devastating than a Saxon sack in general result.

This brings us back to Wroxeter and the bodies found around the Baths in 1860. Many human bones were found, the most dramatic of the discoveries being five skeletons in the hypocausts, one being an old man near whom was found a hoard of coins once contained in a wooden box.[15] The presence of signs of burning and all these bones certainly suggests a disaster, and we have the romantic picture of the old man with his savings and his companions creeping into the hypocausts for safety and there getting suffocated. No one suffering from plague is likely to have acted thus. On the other hand there is no indication in the account that the bath floor was in position, and if they had been robbed later, one would have expected the bones to be disturbed. Could they all be later burials? It is worth recalling that Professor Donald Atkinson found quite a quantity of human remains on the site of the Forum just opposite. These were mainly just odd bones and were thought[16] to be remnants of a post-Roman (?) cemetery more of which was found on Site VI nearby in 1914;[17] but one skeleton lying on the edge of Watling Street was thought to be possibly fifth-century. However, no other traces of destruction by fire were found in any of these later excavations, and we have to keep an open mind when wondering if Wroxeter perished by sack, or by plague, or whether the skeletons were all from quite late burials. The fact that the old man had a hoard of Roman coins going down to Valens does argue against him being medieval.

At Caerwent, too, fire had destroyed the basilica and various shops and houses at a date which must lie well within the fifth century; but life of a sort probably continued long thereafter. This was a part of Britain which was not overrun from the east until the Norman conquest.[18]

Exeter is another western city well beyond the reach of early Saxons. Here the coin list ends with one of Magnus Maximus; no Theodosian issues are recorded, and Lady Fox's excavations showed that pits to contain household rubbish were being cut in the Forum piazza about 380, or soon after, and that the piazza-surface was allowed to become covered with 6-9 inches of wind-blown or rain-washed mould, which itself contained coins going down no later.[19] This in itself might be taken to suggest the breakdown of civic life before the end of the fourth century. But the evidence for it happening so soon is merely the absence of Theodosian issues, for which there might easily be other reasons so far west, for instance if the bulk importation of Theodosian coinage was made by Stilicho for troop payments; and civic life of a sort certainly seems to have continued—that is if the account in the Life of St John the Almsgiver, of an Alexandrian corn ship reaching Britain in the sixth century and returning with a cargo of tin, refers to Exeter. The ship made contact with a certain πρῶτος τῆς πόλεως (rendered *primus civitatis* in Anastasius' later Latin translation) who arranged the exchange because of a local famine. The word πόλις would certainly imply a town, and Exeter is the nearest such πόλις to Cornwall. But Radford's excavations at Castle Dore have shown good reasons for identifying it with the stronghold of King Mark: and I do not feel confident that it was not some such place rather than Exeter to which the corn-ship came:[20] for Exeter is far from the tin-producing area and could only be expected to have tin to trade with if it were still the political centre of Dumnonia. However, in Exeter itself, owing to erosion of the hillside, levels of this date have not survived, or have not so far been identified.

At Silchester there is suggestive evidence bearing on the end of the city. (i) We have the Germanic military equipment, and glass also of fifth-century date, which were published by G. C. Boon.[21] (ii) There are the earthworks studied by O'Neil.[22] He made out quite a convincing case for a sub-Roman *territorium* marked by boundary dykes rather than a defensive perimeter, and suggested that it represented a phase of equilibrium in the relations of Britons with Saxons—a phase such as might have occured after Mount Badon. It is interesting to note how the road to Dorchester-on-Thames has been utterly lost: it crossed a frontier and ceased to be used: while the London road survived long enough to be perpetuated in later boundaries. (iii) The Ogham stone from the well in Insula IX. This is an outlier from the mass of Ogham inscriptions in Ireland and the West; Alcock has suggested[23] that the Ogham script may have been invented at the Irish court of the rulers of Pembrokeshire in the fifth century. As for the Silchester stone we may note—without necessarily believing— Professor Kenneth Jackson's dating of its script on stylistic grounds to about the seventh century, though he does say that the linguistic form could suit a somewhat earlier date.[24] It is difficult to see how anyone could have been living in Silchester, or a well have been open there, in the seventh century. But if the earthworks do mark a phase of equilibrium in the process of Anglo-Saxon settlement, we might well believe that Silchester survived until the middle of the sixth century—until in fact the resumption of the Saxon advance soon after 550—and regard this stone as reinforcing the suggestion.

There are two other towns which I must mention. One is Catterick. This is not a cantonal capital, but it is one of the few towns north of the Humber, and the only one to have produced any relevant evidence. The town wall was built— it is thought—about 300, and it encloses $15\frac{1}{2}$ acres. Within the walls excavation in 1959 by Mr J. S. Wacher showed that rebuilding on a large scale was taking place as late as the 370s, and later still occurred further structural periods which must take us well into the fifth century. At the beginning of the fourth century the Bath building, which had in the second century been part of the *mansio*, was rebuilt but never completed. The wall flues were never inserted nor were the floors or roof. At first sight this seems like a civic set-back; but we cannot tell whether these Baths were intended to be public or whether they, like their predecessors, were built to serve some governmental office which was transferred before the Baths were finished. At any rate, in the later fourth century, after a good deal of domestic refuse had been tipped within the shell, the site was occupied as a dwelling with cobbled floors. The date of this is not exactly fixed. In Insula VII some previously freestanding buildings were linked together by walls, and a monumental entry-arch led into the yard (Fig. 21): the whole complex forming a rather loosely knit unit of some size. The date of this is some-time after 370. The grandiose entrance suggests the public service, whether another *mansio* or possibly the headquarters of a military force, the presence of which is anyhow suggested by the large zoomorphic buckles found by Mr Hildyard[25] in 1952, and now republished by Mrs Hawkes.[26] Across the side-street, in Insula VI, building VI 8 had its open front closed in with an apse about the

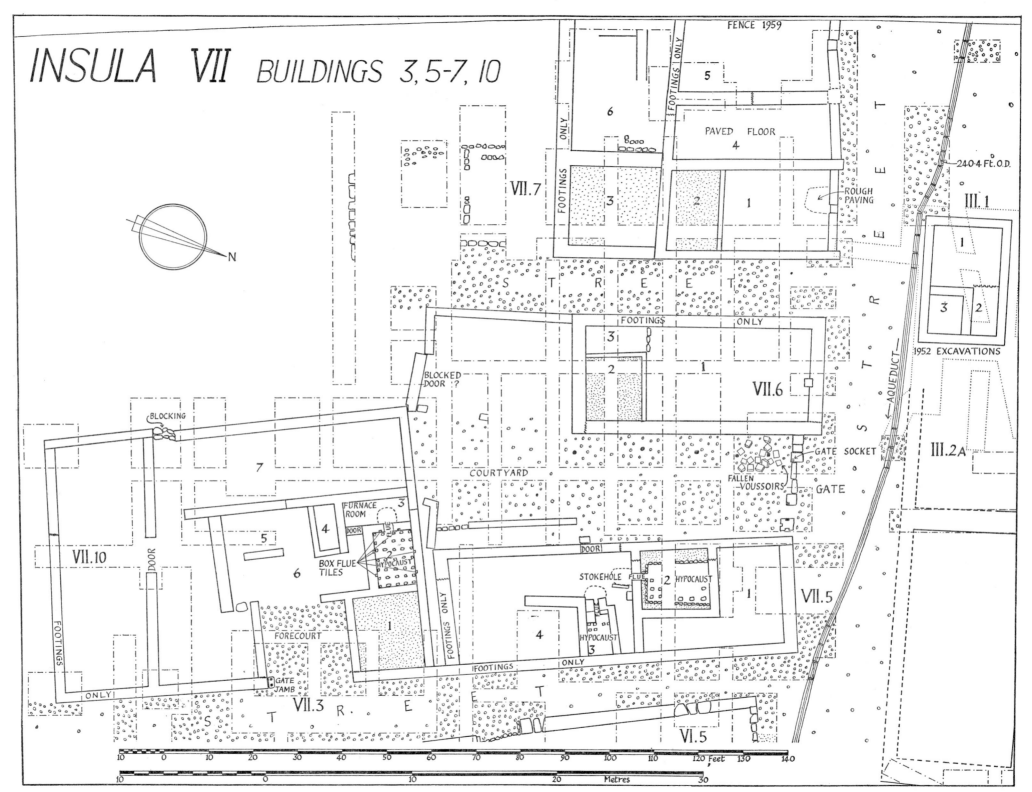

Fig. 21. Plan of late fourth-century compound and other associated buildings at Catterick.
(*Crown copyright*)

same date. The building then remained in use long enough for occupation material to accumulate on its floor, after which it fell into decay: soil accumulated round its walls and over its floor until nothing remained visible. It was only then that a new building was put on the site, and this building was constructed entirely of timber, with individual posts set in the ground or on blocks of stone. This again must clearly be an activity of the fifth century, and traces of similar buildings were found elsewhere, e.g. in Insula III. Thus life continued behind the walls of Catterick in the fifth century, but we cannot tell how long it continued. A few pieces of Saxon pottery were found, but very few— only 5 in the $3\frac{1}{2}$ acres excavated—and it seems clear that by the later sixth century the town as such had ceased to exist. Later Saxon objects are known in the neighbourhood, and a Saxon settlement may have been formed at Catterick village itself. About 590 the British were defeated at a battle usually thought to have been at Catterick: but it is difficult to stretch the life of Roman Cataractonium as late as this, or anything like it.

My last town is Verulamium. Here we have impressive evidence for the continued functioning of town life well into the fifth century, and here the archaeological evidence is confirmed by the facts known of St Germanus' visit to the city in 429, and the assembly there of a well-dressed multitude for a theological debate.[27] The facts are published and need not be described at length.[28] Building XIV 3 was a small house or shop not built until about 370, and thereafter undergoing alterations which take it into the fifth century. Building XXVII 2 gave even clearer evidence. It was a large and prosperous courtyard house, and overlay coins which showed that it too was first constructed after 370. In a second phase, perhaps about 390, some rooms had been enlarged and supplied with big expensive mosaics. Thus at the end of the century there is evidence of prosperity comparable to that suggested by the remains of a house found in Watermoor Road, Cirencester in 1958. These were the homes of wealthy men, the families of a Pelagius or a Gratian; it was to the occupants of such houses that Honorius' rescript was directed. This phase lasted long enough for one of the mosaics to be clumsily patched. Thereafter in a third phase, one of these luxurious rooms was sacrificed to house a corn-drying oven. We may infer that (perhaps c. 410-420) barbarian or peasant disturbances were making the countryside unsafe, and the harvest was hurried within the protection of the town-walls and there treated. The corn-drying furnace had a long life, for its stoke-hole had been reconstructed; it was carefully searched for coins and pottery, but none were found—suggestive evidence of a date nearing 430. Finally the house itself was demolished, and its site occupied by a large hall or barn, whose wall contained a bonding course entirely made of broken fragments of tile. How long this building lasted could not be established; but when finally it in turn had perished, its site was crossed by a pipe-line trench still containing the iron collars for jointing the wooden water-main. That this was later than the barn is shown by the fact that it sliced through one of the latter's buttresses. It would not be wild guesswork to assign this pipe-line to a date around 450; it might indeed be later. The importance of this sequence is that it shows that even at such a late date the urban traditions of the past—clean water, aqueducts, public fountains—were still alive, and so was the craftsmanship which could construct or maintain them. Thus well into the middle of the fifth century Verulamium survived, and how it did so is suggested by the presence in it of a piece of military equipment of the Dorchester type; furthermore the distribution maps show a suggestive absence not only of fifth but also of sixth-century pagan Saxon settlements and cemeteries for many miles round Verulamium (though there are some *-inga* names). A single hut recently discovered at Stevenage is the sole exception. We know that the Chilterns did form a British reserve until the renewal of Saxon conquest in this area in 571. Whether this kingdom was still physically based on Verulamium as late as this it is impossible to say; but certainly the Catuvellauni who then went under were still in some sense the representatives of the traditions which Verulamium had so long inspired.

Thus in one way or another the results of modern excavation, or of survey and research, have shown what Collingwood was unable to show in 1936; that life continued in our towns, often on quite a civilized level, well into the fifth century. But it has also shown that this was possible only by hiring the services of Germanic troops, who sooner or later were likely to rebel. This new fact has meant that a more realistic date, in closer agreement with continental dating of objects, can be given without reservation to the earliest burials in our Saxon cemeteries. The two worlds meet now before 400 in a preliminary phase of co-operative relations before the Saxon settlement proper began.

In Britain this has had to be deduced mainly from archaeological record: we have no full contemporary eye-witness sources. In conclusion I would like to quote one or two short passages from an eye-witness account of parallel events in another part of the Empire: only so can we vividly appreciate what it was all about.

St Severinus[29] came to Noricum Ripense, a province on the upper Danube, after the death of Attila in 452. The *Notitia Dignitatum* mentions a *Dux Pannoniae Primae et Norici Ripensis,* and gives a sizeable list of the forces under his command.[30] By Severinus' time all these had disappeared. What had happened to them is explained (ch. xx). In the old days soldiers used to be paid to guard the frontier; but now this custom had ceased and the military formations had disintegrated. A few only were still in existence and they decided to send some of their number to Italy in search of pay; but these did not get through, being slain by the barbarians on the road.

Instead of regular troops, the only ones available are *foederati*, and they are little use. Foreseeing the destruction of Asturis, St Severinus went on to the next nearest town, Commagenis. This was closely guarded by a force of barbarians billeted in the town who had entered a treaty with the Romans—which means the local provincials—and no one could easily enter or leave the gates. But St Severinus, because he was unknown to them, was neither questioned at the gates nor turned back. This shows the quality of the guard. The third day after he arrived, at the time of the evening service, there was a sudden earth-tremor; the barbarian soldiers panicked, and forced the gates open and fled from the town. In great confusion, they imagined they were being attacked by the enemy, and in the darkness they drew their swords and slaughtered each other. The people of the town looked upon this as a divinely-sent rescue, and for a time continued learning from the Saint to resist with spiritual weapons. Soon, however, the neighbouring town of Favianis was overtaken by a serious famine, and sent for Severinus. A little later an unexpected barbarian raid captured a number of men and cattle outside the walls. The people once again turned to St Severinus, who spoke to the local commander or tribune, Mamertinus, and asked if he had any armed men with whom to pursue the raiders. The tribune replied, "I have indeed a very small number of soldiers, but I dare not engage such a large number of the enemy," but added that, if Severinus advised it, they would trust to his prayers rather than their own arms to bring victory. They then followed up the raiders, who fled, leaving their arms to be collected by the victors.

Soon after St Severinus had left Batava, Hunnimundus at the head of a small barbarian band was able to capture the town while all the inhabitants were at mass and only 40 men were on guard.

The Rugi were the barbarian tribe living on the north bank of the Danube, but in addition to them there were the Alemanni to fear. We are told that the people of Quintana were worn out by the numerous incursions of the Alemanni, and abandoned their city and migrated to Batava: there St Severinus helped them to drive off an Alemannic raid, but then told the combined inhabitants that they must evacuate Batava in turn and take refuge in Lauriacum. By this time the upper half of the province had been abandoned or overrun.

In some ways the situation in Noricum was easier than that in Britain, for the powerful Rugi were Christian, and their king had a high regard for St Severinus, and could often be persuaded by him. This king now advanced on Lauriacum, since it contained all the inhabitants of the empty towns now in his hands, and he wanted to repopulate these towns under his own control. The people of Lauriacum sent St Severinus to meet the king, and he arranged for a pacific (not a forcible) repopulation of the towns on condition that the Rugi would defend them against the Alemanni and other German tribes. In the end, however, in 488, some years after the saint's death, the provincials were withdrawn to Italy.

In this short summary of parts of Eugippius' life of St Severinus, we see happening almost all the alternatives that I discussed in the earlier part of this paper. We have the interruption or breakdown of the supply of pay to the army. We have the Germanic federate garrisons, not much use, given to panic, and not loved by the populace. We have the ineffectiveness of barbarian attempts to capture a walled town unless every one was at mass. We have the lack of determination on the part of the provincials to defend themselves: we have the sack of some towns, the famine at others, and the evacuation of still others. We have the appearance of unofficial leaders, usually saints or bishops, who replace the official leaders like the ineffective tribune. But until the final removal to Italy we have the continued existence of Romanized life of a sort under whatever the difficulties. All this should help us to picture, and to interpret, the end of town life in Roman Britain, and with it the end of Romano-British civilization itself, of which the towns had been both the first instruments and the last bastions.

NOTES

1 Gildas, *de excidio*, § 24.
2 T. Wright, *Uriconium* (1872), 68, 118; *V.C.H.* Salop, 217.
3 *V.C.H.* Hants., 372.
4 C. F. C. Hawkes in (ed.) D. B. Harden, *Dark Age Britain* (1956), 95.
5 *Past and Present*, 14 (Nov. 1958), 2-29.
6 *Med. Arch.*, v, (1961), 1-70.
7 *Arch. J.*, xc, 290, pl. 1.
8 In a lecture to the British Archaeological Association on the Canterbury hoard.
9 J. P. C. Kent, "From Roman Britain to Saxon England" in R. H. M. Dolley, *Anglo-Saxon Coins*, 2.
10 *J.R.S.*, xxi, 232; *Arch. J.*, cvi, 65.
11 R. Rainbird Clarke, *East Anglia* (1960), 130.
12 *Med.Arch.*, vi, 1-15.
13 *Antiq. J.*, xliii, 21-2.
14 C. E. Stevens, *E.H.R.*, lvi (1941), 363.
15 T. Wright, *Uriconium* (1872), 68, 118-19.
16 D. Atkinson, *Wroxeter 1923-27* (1942), 112.
17 J. P. Bushe-Fox, *Wroxeter 1914*, 19.
18 A. Fox in *A Hundred Years of Welsh Archaeology* (Cambrian Archaeological Association Centenary Volume, 1846-1946), 107.
19 A. Fox, *Roman Exeter* (1952), 24, 41.
20 Migne, *Patrologia Graeca* XCIII (1625): *Vita Sancti Ioannis Eleemosynarii*, ix; Leontius' original text, (ed.) H. Gelzer, Leipzig 1893.
21 *Med.Arch.*, iii (1959), 79-88.
22 *Antiquity*, xviii (1944), 133 ff.
23 *Celtic Studies in Wales* (1963), 42-4.
24 *Med. Arch.*, iii, 87.
25 *Y.A.J.*, xxxix (1957), 243 ff.
26 *Med.Arch.*, v, 43, 62.
27 Bede, *H.E.*, I, 17-18.
28 *Antiq. J.*, xl, 19-21; *Bull.Inst.Arch.*, iv, 69; *Antiquity*, xxxvii, 103.
29 *Monumenta Germaniae Historica* I; Eugippius, *Vita Sancti Severini*.
30 *Not.Dig.Occ.*, xxxiv.

SUMMING-UP: SOME HISTORICAL ASPECTS OF THE CIVITATES OF ROMAN BRITAIN

by

A. L. F. Rivet

CONFERENCE of this kind does not lend itself to a formal summing-up; what is new requires digestion, which can only be achieved after publication, what is old has already been considered elsewhere. Since the majority of speakers have dealt with individual cities or with particular facets of their life, it may be more useful if, by way of conclusion, we stand back and try to view the subject in a wider perspective. Accordingly an attempt is made here to set the development of the tribal cities in their historical context, paying due attention to those aspects of the matter which have been fully discussed, but concentrating especially on those which have not.

Among the latter the most important is the question of the native background, and we may conveniently begin with the earliest literary reference to British tribal organization. This is the statement of Diodorus Siculus that the Britons "have many kings and rulers and for the most part they live at peace with one another."[1] Whether this really derives, as is sometimes supposed, from Pytheas or, perhaps more probably, from Caesarian sources, it may fairly be taken as describing the state of affairs in pre-Belgic, or at least non-Belgic, Britain. Though the peace might seem to have been an armed one, the multiplicity of rulers is surely reflected in our very numerous hill-forts. It is, indeed, just what we should expect, given the geographical position of Britain and the archaeological evidence of successive infiltrations.

In Caesar's own writings we can see that, under the impact of Belgic influences, this old fragmentary society was already in process of change, but the change had not yet been completed and there were still four kings in so small an area as Kent.[2] Further, Caesar mentions a number of tribal names,[3] and although the Trinovantes are familiar to us from later sources, the others are not; the Cenimagni may possibly represent the Iceni, but for the Segontiaci, the Ancalites, the Bibroci, and the Cassi this is their only appearance on the stage of British history. The older antiquaries used to pay these tribes quite a lot of attention, locating them with confidence and even deriving place-names from them. The fact that they are now properly out of sight on the map does not mean that we should put them altogether out of mind. They may yet prove to be of interest, not only in the early period, when some of them may well have been among the *civitates Cogidubno regi donatae,*[4] but, remembering the re-emergence of tribes like the Catalauni in Gaul, in the later period too.

They have certainly disappeared by the time we come to our next comprehensive reference. This is Ptolemy's Geography which, though it was compiled in the second century, can be shown to rely mainly on first-century material. Here, instead of a multiplicity of small tribes we find that a limited number of federations or super-states have emerged. In Roman terms, presumably the smaller and weaker tribes had become clients of the larger and stronger, sacrificing their independent deterrents for peace and, they must have hoped, for prosperity. That is one way of looking at it. Another way is to see in the change something analogous to what the Greeks called συνοικισμός, the coming together of scattered people to form viable states. Whether it was forced or voluntary, it was evidently this process that created the basis for the Roman organization of Britain. Thanks mainly to the work of Mr Derek Allen we no longer have to rely on a straight comparison of Caesar and Ptolemy. The distributions of the tribal coinages define with remarkable clarity political units that correspond closely with the Ptolemaic tribes.[5] Some Roman adjustments are indeed detectable, such as the creation of the Regnenses from the southern Atrebates and perhaps the attribution of some of the Dobunni to the Belgae, but the general pattern is clearly the result of pre-Roman evolution.

Before we proceed further, there are two features of these pre-Roman states that merit attention. We have considered them as unions, but this does not necessarily mean that they were unities and in fact in almost every case there is evidence of division. So far as individuals are concerned, we do not know the precise political relationship of Cunobelin and Epaticcus, but we do know that Togodumnus and Caratacus were both leaders of the Catuvellauni after them, we know of the later strife between Venutius and Cartimandua, and a schism has been suggested between Bodvoc and Corio among the Dobunni.[6] Geographically it may be seen in the distribution of mints and *oppida*. Thus Verulamium was not given up when the Catuvellauni took over Camulodunon, the Atrebates had mints at both Silchester and Selsey, the Coritani seem to have had centres at both Leicester and Old Sleaford,[7] and for the Dobunni Minchinhampton may rival Bagendon. Nor need this surprise us. Caesar stresses the existence of the same sort of thing in Gaul, where division was considered to be a safeguard against tyranny: *omnes civitates in partis divisae sunt duas*—and he gives instances of its operation.[8]

The second feature is the nature of the administrative centres of the superstates. These are not hill-forts in the accepted sense of the word, but sprawling low-lying settlements, and some of them are very large indeed. The area of Belgic Camulodunon is much greater than that of the Roman *colonia* which was inserted in it and native Corinion (for that is surely the name of the Bagendon site, beside the river Churn) seems also to have been larger than the Roman city of Corinium. Minchinhampton is on the same scale. Professor Frere's discovery of mint material down beside the Ver[9] extends the area of Verulamium far beyond Prae Wood, and he has in the course of this conference suggested that Belgic Canterbury too was larger than its Roman successor. What went on in these vast areas remains obscure : they are large enough for training troops holding durbars, growing crops and rounding up cattle. The point is that although they cannot properly be called cities, some of the Britons were already accustomed to central settlements on a truly regal scale.

Then came the Claudian invasion. With characteristic directness, the main thrust was made against the largest and most powerful of the states, the Catuvellauni and their capital at Camulodunon, and the immediate results of the initial Roman victories are themselves interesting. The Catuvellaunian empire began to fall apart and various subject tribes came to terms with the invader. The first to do so were some of the 'Bodunni', whose identity with the Dobunni has been finally demonstrated by Professor Hawkes.[10] But note that it is not the whole tribe of the Dobunni, but part of them—μέρος τι τῶν Βοδούννων— for they are, as we have already noted, fissile.

After the first campaigns followed the consolidation. In recent years we have acquired a much improved picture of the early stages of the occupation, and the leading worker in this field, Dr Graham Webster, has given the conference a stimulating review of the evidence as it stands now. In the present context the most significant point that emerges is the distribution pattern of the early forts and its similarity to the distribution, which was already familiar to us, of forts in Wales. For in both cases the pattern is less that of a frontier in the true sense of the word than of a holding system. Ideally, the conquest of a province like Britain had three phases : first, the actual war of conquest, which is likely to be reflected archaeologically, if at all, by camps rather than by forts; second, a phase of consolidation, marked by these forts, in which it was made clear that Roman rule was for ever; and third, a civil phase when, the denarius having dropped, the inhabitants settled down to sensible Roman life in towns and the garrisons could be withdrawn. One might indeed go so far as to regard those forts as successful which could finally be abandoned, and those as failures where, as in Wales and the north, the garrisons had to be maintained or, even if they could be withdrawn, nothing that could be called civilized supervened. But the starting point was the same in both cases, and for them to be effective as a holding system, the siting of the forts must have taken account not merely of tactical military requirements but also of political strategy, so that a coincidence between native settlement and early Roman fort is to be expected. In any case it is clear from the work of Dr Webster and others that many of these early forts, or the trading settlements attached to them (whether or not they had native antecedents), did form the nuclei of future towns.

But what sort of towns were they? While not all of them were in the class we are considering, this is the point at which we become involved in 'cantonal capitals', or 'tribal cities', as such. It is not appropriate here to go into the minutiae of the legal position; not only have we had a paper on the subject from Miss Reynolds, but it has recently been debated, in the pages of *Antiquity*, by

Professor Frere and Dr Mann.[11] Nevertheless, there are some generally agreed facts which can with advantage be restated and one or two aspects of the debate which seem to call for comment. The agreed facts are these: first, the legal form taken by the tribal constitutions would have depended on the original treaties made by Claudius, and other emperors, with the British tribes. We do not know what any of them said, and especially in view of the personality of Claudius there is likely to have been a good deal of variation in them, but they are still likely to have followed precedent elsewhere. Second, to judge from the precedents available, and from such epigraphic evidence as we have, some system of indirect rule was normally applied; that is to say, the day-to-day administration of the tribal units was left in the hands of the tribal aristocracy. Third, whatever system was actually used, it had to deliver the goods, in the form of tribute and taxes and army recruits. This does not rule out the possibility of high-minded idealism in the men who administered the system—no doubt Agricola, for example, had plenty of it—but it does help to define the position of the tribal notables. Caesar used to take hostages, and although Claudius, faced with different problems, used different methods, it is hardly an exaggeration to say that these people, whether as *decuriones* or *duoviri* or *vergobrets,* were in a sense hostages for the good behaviour of their tribe.

But to be effective, both economically and politically, the tribal unit had to have a centre, a recognized metropolis. In *Antiquity,* Professor Frere quoted a passage from Strabo on the Allobriges: "Formerly the Allobriges kept up warfare with many myriads of men, but they now cultivate the plains and glens in the Alps, and all of them live in villages, except that the most notable of them, dwelling in Vienne (formerly itself a village but called nevertheless the metropolis of the tribe) have built it up into a city."[12] He pointed out that κώμη, the Greek word which Strabo uses for 'village' is exactly equivalent to the Latin word *vicus,* and then concluded: "Vienne, then ranked as a *vicus.*" But both κώμη and *vicus* have an everyday as well as a legal meaning, and the fact that Strabo uses an adverb, κωμηδόν, to express 'in villages' suggests that it is the non-technical sense that is in the front of his mind. Surely all he is doing is voicing the sentiment that any Roman citizen would share, whether he came from Pontus or Forum Julii, and saying: "Well done, Allobriges, you are learning about civilization." And this surely is what our man from Forum Julii was after when he encouraged the Britons to build *templa fora domos.* The city is the sine qua non of civilization. Note that Tacitus is referring specifically to the tribal capitals, which are the only places, apart from *coloniae,* where we find *fora.*[13]

Secondly, there is the intended relationship of these places to the tribal territory. "The tribes of Narbonensis," wrote Professor Frere, "were still sufficiently small to be treated as city states, or became so when the foundations of Caesarian colonies partitioned their territory. But north of this the tribal areas were so vast as to make such treatment ludicrously out of scale."[14] It is, of course, true that many of the Gaulish and British tribal territories were too large for their organization to be modelled closely on that of a Roman *colonia,* but the Roman *colonia* is not the only form of city state. In this particular respect it is instructive to seek comparisons in the home of the city state, in Greece itself. Here there are some cities, like Megara and Sicyon, with very small, *colonia*-sized, territories, but the area of Attica is very similar to that of our own Cantiaci, and the distance from Athens to Sunium is the same as that from Canterbury to Rochester. Indeed looking at the case of Athens and Sparta, and comparing it with that of Sicyon and Megara, one might conclude that the possession of a substantial territory was essential to success. Nor are the Narbonese tribes themselves so very small. Strabo stresses the size of the Volcae Arecomici, who stretched from Nîmes to Narbonne, a distance of 88 Roman miles,[15] while even in the Rhône valley Miss Reynolds has reminded us of the extent of theVocontii, whose two tribal centres are 40 miles apart.

These two points have little bearing on the legal argument itself, but they do clear the way for a restatement of two practical points. First, the Romans, with their own traditions of civilized life, actually thought it right that the Britons too should have cities which could be recognized as such; in this respect Agricola's intentions are made quite clear by Tacitus. Second, there was no objection on grounds of scale to their encouraging the Britons, not to say compelling them, to build metropoleis that were in a very real sense the centres of their tribal areas; and all the archaeological evidence, such as has been presented to this conference, does indicate that a special effort was put into them, especially in the matter of monumental buildings.

One further aspect of the relationship of the cities to their surroundings deserves mention. A few years ago, in a different context, I plotted the distribution of villas in relation to towns, erecting them into groups.[16] A curious fact emerged from this exercise, that in almost every case the largest groups occur not round the tribal capital but round a secondary town. Thus Rochester has more villas than Canterbury, Mildenhall more than Silchester, and so on. The implication of this seems to be that, at least for a time, the land around the capitals was worked actually from the towns, just as it was from the *coloniae.* Where villas do occur very near to a city, as at Barton Farm near Cirencester or at Olga Road near Dorchester, they tend to be late. This is a subject that might repay further attention, because it bears on the deliberation with which these places were founded, and any future conference might well include a paper on suburbs.

Once founded, the cities had a complicated history; the overwhelming impression one gets from this conference is just how complicated it was. Mr Wacher's study of earthwork defences has shown that the full story of their delimitation, their defences, and their expansion and contraction, is still very far from being understood. But although we are not yet at the end of the

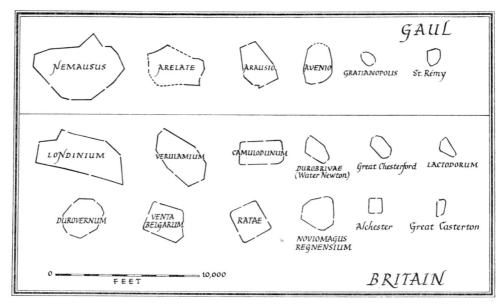

Fig. 22. Comparative sizes of walled towns in Gaul and Britain.

argument about the date, or rather dates, of even the actual walls, one thing remains clear, even after Mr Wacher's modifications: the towns of Britain, with few exceptions, were walled earlier than the towns of Gaul. This makes direct comparison with Gaul difficult, but it does mean that we can get a picture of the approximate size of our towns in their heyday. And in the very few cases where comparisons can be drawn, the British towns show up surprisingly well (Fig. 22). Thus although Nîmes is larger than London, several of our cities (Verulamium, Wroxeter, Cirencester) compare favourably with places like Arles and Orange and Avignon. This is the early Arles, not the later shrunken version, and when one recalls how much of Orange is taken up by an impossible hill, the comparison is still more favourable. But there is more to it than that. On the right of the figure are two examples which are fairly typical of late towns in Gaul: St Rémy, which succeeded Glanum when it had been sacked by barbarians, and Grenoble, which, as Gratianopolis, succeeded the more extensive Cularo. Below them, still on the same scale, are some of our own small towns.

There is food for thought here, because this shrinkage in Gaul, after the barbarian invasions, applies to tribal capitals as well as to minor towns.[17] Several factors were involved, religious as well as secular, but the most important one seems to have been that in this late period the authorities decided that they could do without the huge monumental buildings—the *templa* and the *fora*—which had been their pride in earlier days, and they were not restored. So fragments

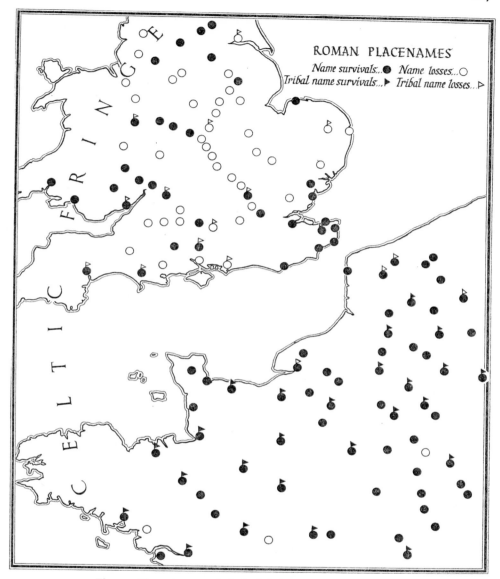

Fig. 23. Place-name survivals in Britain and north-west Gaul.

of venerable monuments were built into the footings of the new town walls and at places like Périgueux and Tours sections of the amphitheatre were actually incorporated in them as they stood. The late walls of Périgueux enclose 14 acres, those of Tours 23; for comparison, the walled area of Durobrivae (Water

Newton) is 44 acres, that of Great Chesterford 37, and that of Alchester 27. It is clear that in a late context, when *templa* and *fora* could be dispensed with, very many of our smaller towns would have been acceptable as administrative centres.

To understand the full significance of this, it is necessary first to look briefly at one form of evidence which we have so far neglected, that of names. As is well known, in Gaul virtually all the tribal capitals are not only named with tribal suffixes, but actually have the tribal suffix converted into the name, so that it is the name of the tribe, not that of the place, that has survived into medieval and modern times; just how universal this is may be seen from reference to the map (Fig. 23). In Britain, however, the story is quite different. With the possible exception of Canterbury, such few names as did survive are derived from the name of the town, not that of the tribe. This is often assumed, perhaps rightly, to be no more than a side-effect of the different forms taken by the barbarian occupation;[18] certainly the breakdown of the Roman organization was more complete in Britain, and the failure of the British bishoprics to maintain continuity must also be taken into account. Nevertheless, it seems worth while to consider whether there is any evidence that the divergence had its roots in an earlier period.

The epigraphic evidence on this point is meagre in the extreme and with one exception quite uninformative,[19] but the other documentary evidence for place-names must at least be reviewed. In Ptolemy, whose sources for Britain are mainly of Flavian date, all the tribal capitals are mentioned except Venta Silurum,[20] but they are not distinguished in any way from other towns in the same tribal area, nor are the proprietary formulae, ὧν πόλις and καὶ πόλις αὐτῶν, which are normal in Gaul, ever employed; but this is probably not significant, since Ptolemy's usage varies widely from province to province. In the Ravenna Cosmography, which in Britain seems to refer mainly to the second century,[21] tribal suffixes are applied to all the capitals which are mentioned (except Verulamium and Petuaria, which may be accepted as special cases), but by an unlucky chance Isurium and Durnovaria are omitted altogether. The case of the Antonine Itinerary is very complicated. It is reasonable to regard the date of some of it as early third century,[22] but there have been many later amendments, and in the British section at least two strains are evident.[23] These cannot be distinguished by date, however, and we can only take the work as a whole. Here Calleva Atrebatum, Venta Belgarum, Isurium Brigantum, Isca Dumnoniorum, Venta Icenorum, and Venta Silurum all appear at least once with suffixes, while in Icinos and perhaps Regnum we have only examples in Britain of pure tribal names. But there are no suffixes for Durovernum, Verulamium, Ratae, Durnovaria, and Viroconium (though this last is not quite certain).[24] Again disregarding Verulamium, this gives a score of 6 or 7 with suffixes to 3 or 4 without, which would be increased to 5 or 6 without if we took in the marginal cases of Petuaria for the Parisi and Moridunum for the Demetae. At first sight this looks suggestive, but the comparable score for the part of Gaul shown on the map is 7 to 9 (12 are not mentioned in the Itinerary at all), so that no valid conclusions can be drawn from it alone. The Peutinger Table may also be taken as representing the third century, perhaps more consistently than the Itinerary, though it too has been revised and in parts Christianized. Only three of our tribal cities appear on the surviving portion and of these Isca Dumnoniorum and Venta Icenorum (as . . . ta . . . um) have suffixes, but Durovernum has not; no meaningful comparisons can be made with Gaul. Finally, in our last authority, the *Notitia Dignitatum,* the one British city which is mentioned appears not as Venta Belgarum but as plain Venta—which is what we should expect, to give us Winchester, not Belchester.

There remains the exceptional piece of epigraphic evidence. This consists of the wall inscriptions of the Durotrages (or Durotroges) Lindinienses (or Lendinienses), from which Mr Stevens has been able to demonstrate that the tribal area of the Durotriges was partitioned between Ilchester (Lindinis) and Dorchester (Durnovaria).[25] If the stones refer to the Severan reconstruction of the wall, as seems likely, this case would indeed be unusual in occuring so early,[26] but there is no reason to suppose that it may not have been repeated elsewhere in Britain at a later date. To take only the 'tribeless' names in the Antonine Itinerary, Durnovaria is already accounted for and there are towns to hand with which the power of the others might, in a late context, be shared: Rochester for the Cantiaci, Alchester and Water Newton[27] for the Catuvellauni, perhaps Margidunum for the Coritani, and Wall for the Cornovii. If this happened, the people inhabiting the towns would become known not by tribal names but as Durnovarienses (Dorchester), Durobrivenses (Rochester), Durovernenses (Canterbury), Letocetenses (Wall), and Viroconienses (Wroxeter)—in most of these cases simplifying the origins of their later names. Moreover these names would apply not only to the town but to its territory too, which could explain how the name of Letocetum could be transferred from Wall to Lichfield, how the Magnenses of Kenchester could give rise to the Magonsaetas and how Paulinus could set up his cross *in Cambodono* at Dewsbury (which cannot itself be the Cambodunum of the Itinerary because it is not on the main road that is being followed). And if the church in fourth-century Britain had adjusted its organization to that of the secular power, the establishment of Justus as Bishop of Rochester in 604 becomes more readily intelligible. The 28 *civitates* of Gildas and Nennius may not be so mythical as we sometimes assume.

Of course all this is highly speculative, but if there is a possibility that widespread fragmentation of territories occurred in the later stages of Roman Britain, it carries some interesting implications. Did the lines of cleavage correspond at all with the intratribal divisions which we noted at the beginning? Are we looking for the right name-survivals in the right places? How far is evidence of decline in one of the recognized tribal cities a reliable indicator of the fortunes of how wide a territory? Certainly it draws attention to a fundamental fact which Professor Richmond stated at the very beginning of the Conference: the various aspects of Roman Britain are interdependent. If we wish to know more about the tribal cities, we must find out more about the other towns too.

Indeed, looking at this Conference, as we must look at it, as a guide to what most needs doing in the future, I would put the study of the other towns very high on the list, especially places like Water Newton and Alchester, which are both large and accessible. Also high on the list I would put the study of buildings, both inside and outside the towns, not as a substitute for the investigation of town walls, but as an essential supplement to it. It has not been neglected at places like Verulamium, Wroxeter, and Cirencester, but it could still be pursued more widely, again in the smaller towns as well as in the great cities; we know virtually nothing about their administration, whether or not they achieved promotion. With this goes the study of suburbs, essential to our understanding of the changing fortunes of the towns; here one recalls especially Mr Holmes's demonstration that at Chichester, as at Silchester, the street grid once extended beyond the line later taken by the town walls. And finally, one of the most important tasks of all seems to me to be the study of survivals. Here Professor Frere's masterly survey should be an invaluable stimulant.

This is a suitable note on which to conclude, for two reasons. First, these towns that we have been considering, whether we call them cantonal capitals or tribal cities or just metropoleis, were at once the chief means and the chief result of the Romanization—which in this context means the civilization—of Britain. They are the guarantee that Britain at one time formed an integral part of the Roman world, in their prime representing the success of Roman policy, in their decay its failure, so that the study of them has something to contribute to the history of the Roman Empire. But secondly, it also has something to contribute to the history of Britain. We have all read, and been irritated by, histories of England, sometimes by otherwise reputable historians, which either dismiss the Roman period too briefly or, even if they give it longer treatment, present it as an episode (what in Edinburgh has come to be called a 'happening') which was quite without any effect on what followed after. Neither of these attitudes can be logically sustained: Roman Britain extended over 400 years and history does not happen in chapters. But we ourselves are not always above criticism. We too must first see our period historically, considering all the possibilities of change and development in these four centuries, and, looking both backwards to the Iron Age and forwards to the Saxon kingdoms, seek out the material that is needed for a better understanding of the continuity which must be there.

NOTES

[1] Diodorus Siculus, V, 21. βασιλεῖς τε καὶ δυνάστας πολλοὺς ἔχειν καὶ πρὸς ἀλλήλους κατὰ τὸ πλεῖστον εἰρηνικῶς διακεῖσθαι.

[2] Caesar, *B.G.*, V, 22.

[3] Caesar, *B.G.*, V, 21.

[4] Tacitus, *Agricola*, 14, 2.

[5] See especially *O.S. Map of Southern Britain in the Iron Age* (1962), text map 6, showing Durotriges, Coritani, Iceni, and Dobunni.

[6] E. M. Clifford, *Bagendon, a Belgic Oppidum* (1961), 55-56 (C. F. C. Hawkes) and 101-102 (D. F. Allen). But see also my review, *Antiquity*, xxxvi (1962), 145-7.

[7] D. F. Allen, *Sylloge of the Coins of the British Isles: The Coins of the Coritani* (1963), 19 (for the mint at Old Sleaford), 28-32 (for the suggestion that the inscriptions on the coins represent pairs of magistrates).

[8] Caesar, *B.G.*, VI, 11. While this may normally imply no more than political parties, it was always liable to lead to actual geographical division, as in the case of the Eburones (*B.G.*, VI, 31, *Catuvolcus, rex dimidiae partis Eburonum*). This in turn might mark the beginning of a complete split, such as that which produced the adjacent Aulerci Eburovices, Aulerci Diablintes, and Aulerci Cenomani. It is a somewhat different process from that which produced the wider dispersion of tribal names (Volcae, Bituriges, Brigantes, Cornovii, etc.), for which Livy, V, 34 gives a plausible form of explanation. Mr Charles Thomas tells me that the dual principle is also discernible among the later Picts.

[9] S. S. Frere, *Antiq. J.*, xxxvii (1957), 6.

[10] Cassius Dio, LX, 20. On the statement ἦσαν δὲ οὐκ αὐτόνομοι ἀλλ᾿ ἄλλοις βασιλεῦσι προστεταγμένοι, see C. F. C. Hawkes in *Bagendon*, 60.

[11] J. C. Mann, *Antiquity*, xxxiv (1960), 222; S. S. Frere, *ibid.*, xxxv (1961), 29; J. C. Mann, *ibid.*, 142. For the status of individual tribes one would naturally look to Pliny, but his account of Britain (*N.H.*, iv, 102-104) is vague, out of date and devoid of political detail. Nevertheless a partial classification may be attempted, employing the categories he uses elsewhere :

1. *Coloniae.* Camulodunum, as a veteran colony, would be a full *Colonia Civium Romanorum*, though with *incolae* added. The same should apply to Lindum and Glevum, when founded, but not necessarily to Eburacum which, if it antedated the Constitutio Antoniniana, may only have had *Ius Latii*.

2. *Municipia.* Verulamium must surely have been not a *Municipium Civium Romanorum* but, like Salpensa and Malaca (*I.L.S.* 6088 and 6089), a town with *Ius Latii*, by which magistrates received citizenship. The grant, which may well have been made by Claudius, must have been earned by a co-operative attitude to Rome. It is tempting to link this with the name of Adminius, whose *clientela* could then be localized.

3. *Civitates Foederatae.* The obvious candidates for this grade are the Dobunni, Iceni, Regnenses, and Brigantes (and, at a later date, the Votadini), for the following reasons :

(a) The Dobunni, because they (or at least a part of them) had voluntarily come to terms. As Professor Hawkes has pointed out (*Bagendon* 66), they must be among the *socii* of *Annals* xii, 37 (in A.D. 47); since no revolt is recorded, it is difficult to see why they should have been more hardly dealt with than the Iceni.

(b) The Iceni and Regnenses. Classification of these as 'client kingdoms' obscures the issue; the survival of monarchy was one of the archaic features of British society and need not have affected the relationship of the tribes to Rome, especially when Claudius was her representative. Since Cogidubnus remained *fidissimus*, the Regnenses probably kept the status after his death. The Iceni were evidently *foederati* in A.D. 47 and although they broke their *foedus* by revolting they retained a degree of independence. The appointment of Prasutagus may well date from then (cf. Dudley and Webster, *The Rebellion of Boudicca* (1962), 47) and the appropriate grade for this intermediate stage might be that of a *civitas libera* (i.e. 'free' at Rome's discretion); this would explain the apparently casual way in which their privileges were revoked when Prasutagus died. After the Boudiccan revolt they must certainly have been reduced to a *civitas stipendiaria*.

(c) The Brigantes. While they were still outside the province 'client kingdom' is appropriate and the status of *civitas foederata* seems likely thereafter—at least until the affair of the Genunian Region (Pausanias, *Descr. Graec.*, viii, 43), when it would explain their comparative freedom of action.

4. *Civitates Liberae*. As suggested above, this may have been the intermediate status of the Iceni.

5. *Civitates Stipendiariae*. Positive indications are available in six cases, and take two forms:

(a) The Cantiaci and Belgae, because they seem to have been artificial creations.

(b) The Trinovantes, Durotriges, Silures, and Ordovices, because of their stubborn resistance. The Trinovantes may, indeed, have been attributed to Camulodunum, just as the 24 *ignobilia oppida* of the Volcae Arecomici were attributed to Nemausus.

For the rest—Atrebates, Coritani, Cornovii, Deceangli, Demetae, and Dumnonii—there is no evidence, but the stipendiary grade was the most common. This is illustrated in the following table, where the figures for Gaul are taken from Pliny's account (*N.H.*, iv, 106-109):

	Coloniae	*Municipia*	*Civitates Foederatae*	*Civitates Liberae*	*Civitates Stipendiariae*
Aquitania	0	0	0	4	44
Belgica	3	0	2	4	26
Lugdunensis	1	0	2	2	22
Britannia	1	1	4(3)		12(13)

12 Strabo, IV, 1, 11 (C. 186). *Antiquity*, xxxv (1961), 32.

13 Tacitus, *Agricola*, 21, 1. *Templa*, too, must refer primarily to official structures, especially to the shrines of tutelary deities which, as at Bordeaux (Boudiga) and Périgueux (Vesunna) took the place of a capitol and, adjoining the Forum, formed part of the official plan. It is unfortunate that the best-known town plan in Britain, that of Silchester, is atypical in this respect. For a review of Gaulish examples, see Grenier, *Manuel d'Archéologie Gallo-Romaine*, III, 1958, Part 1 (*l'Urbanisme, les Monuments : Capitole, Forum, Temple, Basilique*). The *domos*, of course, are town-houses, not villas.

14 *Antiquity*, xxxv (1962), 29.

15 Strabo, IV, 1, 12 (C. 186). The distance is stated in IV, 1, 3 (C. 178).

16 (ed) P. Corder, *Romano-British Villas : Some Current Problems* (C.B.A. Research Report No. 1 = *Archaeological News Letter*, vi) (1955), 31.

17 For further examples, see R. M. Butler "Late Roman Town Walls in Gaul", *Arch. J.*, cxvi (1959), 25-50.

18 In this connection it is interesting to note in Britain the very high percentage of survivals among the names of the Saxon Shore forts—Branodunum as Bramcestria, Brancaster; Othona as Ythancaestir; Regulbium as Reculf, Reculver; Rutupiae as Reptacaestir, Retesbrough, Richborough; Portus Dubris as Dofras, Dover; Portus Lemanis as Liminaea, Lympne; Anderita as Andredescester and in Andredes Leag. The river names may have helped Dover and Lympne, but it is tempting to suppose that the transition to English was helped by the presence in them of Germanic-speaking soldiers while still under Roman control. Could the Cnobher of Cnobheresburg, Burgh Castle, the only fort apart from Walton Castle which is missing, have been a federate leader?

19 The Hadrianic milestone inscription 'a Ratis' (*C.I.L.*, vii, 1169) has no particular significance, since the stone was presumably erected by the Coritani themselves; the Calleva stone (*E.E.*, ix, 985-6) and the diploma giving the domicile of Novantico as 'Ratis' (*A.E.*, lvi (1944), No. 57) have already been referred to by Miss Reynolds (p. 73). But all of these are earlier than the Antonine Itinerary and probably than the Ravenna Cosmography. For the Durotriges Lindinienses, see below, note 25.

[20] This omission is itself an indication of early date; the only πόλις given in the territory of the Silures is Βούλλαιον = Burrium, the Roman fort at Usk. More conclusive is the listing of the Flavian forts in the north and the absence of any reference to Hadrian's Wall. Only the legions have been brought up to date.

[21] As indicated by the itemising of the Antonine Wall, I. A. Richmond and O. G. S. Crawford, "The British Section of the Ravenna Cosmography", *Arch.*, xciii (1949), Nos. 191-200. The *diversa loca*, Nos. 228-235, are listed separately and are evidently taken from a later source.

[22] Assuming that the Antoninus Augustus of the title is Caracalla. See D. van Berchem in *Mémoires de la Société Nationale des Antiquaires de France*, lxxix (8th series, ix) (1935), 166-181.

[23] This is especially clear in the contrast between 'Iter V' (474, 1 to 476, 6), which has 'Colonia' and 'Icinos', and 'Iter IX' (479, 10 to 480, 8), which has 'Camoloduno' and 'Venta Icinorum', but the variation in stations between Carlisle and Brough and between London and Canterbury may also indicate differences of date.

[24] The form Viroconiorum (482, 9) suggests either that the scribe was expecting a genitive plural or, more probably, that he has conflated Viroconium Cornoviorum.

[25] *C.I.L.*, vii, 695; *E.E.*, vii, 1052; C. E. Stevens, E.H.R., lvi (1941), 359 and *P.Som.A.N.H.S.*, xcvi, (1952), 188.

[26] For a possible explanation, see I. A. Richmond, *Roman Britain* (2nd edn. 1963), 79.

[27] This is an exceptionally good candidate, as it had mileages measured from it—*C.I.L.*, vii, 1156 = *E.E.*, ix, 634 (milestone of Florian, with the mileage figure I); cf. the stone of Victorinus, with no mileage figure but from the same place, F. J. Haverfield, *Roman Britain in 1913*, 32.

INDEX

Abonae, *see* Sea Mills
Adminius, 111 n.11 (2)
Ad Pontem, *see* Thorpe by Newark
Aedui, 75 n.32
Africa, mosaics 82; markets 84
Agedincum (Sens), France, 74
Agricola, Cn. Julius, on linguistic ability of
   Britons, 19; policy 51, 53, 104-5
air-photographs, —photography, 21-30, 35, 39,
   42, 82
Albinus, Clodius, 57, 67
Alcester, Warwicks., streets 24; fort? 41;
   defences 63
Alchester, Oxon., air-photography 21, 82;
   streets 24; fort? 41; rampart? 62; shops 82;
   size 108, 110; status 82, 109
Alcock, L., 96
Aldborough (Isurium Brigantum), Yorks., air-
   photography 21; pottery 56; fort? 56; dating
   57; rampart 63, 65, 67; status 108
Alemanni, 99
Alexandrian corn-ship, 95
Alfoldean, Sussex, 22
Allen, Derek, 102, 111 nn.6, 7
Allobriges, 104
Ammianus Marcellinus, 52-3
amphitheatres, 84, 107
amphorae, 51 n.9; 54
amulets, 83
Anastasius, 95
Ancalites, 101
Ancaster (Causennae), Lincs., air-photography
   21; fort 35; defences 35, 63
Anderita, *see* Pevensey
Anglesey, Isle of, 32
Anglo-Frisian pottery, settlements, 91-4; Figs.
   18, 19, 20
Anglo-Saxon Chronicle, 87, 93
Anglo-Saxon villages, 92, 96
Anker, river, re. military and civil sites at Man-
   cetter 38
Annable, K., 45 n.79
Antonine, fort at Littlechester 37; pottery 54
— Itinerary, 22, 108-9, 112 n.19
— Wall, 113 n.21
Aosta (Augusta Praetoria), Italy, 71
Aquae Sulis, *see* Bath
aqueducts, 79, 98
Aquitania, Civitates of, 112 n.11
Arcadius, coins of, 93
Arles (Arelate), France, 106
artillery platforms (*see* also bastions), 52

artist, craftsman, native, 19; craftsmanship 98
Atacini, 71
Atkinson, Professor D., 29 n.3, 57 n.8, 58 nn.
   13, 16; 86 nn.11, 47; 95
Atrebates, territory, status 23, 31, 102, 108,
   112 n.11 (5b)
Attila, 98
attributi, 71, 74
Aulerci Eburovices
   „   Diablintes } 111 n.8
   „   Cenomani
Ausonius, 83
Autun (Augustodunum), France, 75 n.32
Avenches (Aventicum), Switzerland, 71, 75 n.4
Aventicum, *see* Avenches
Avignon (Avenio), France, 106
Avon, river, as *limes* 31; re. Cave's Inn 42
Bagendon, Glos., 102
Baker, Arnold, 35, 39, 44 n.47
bakeries, London 79; Silchester 81
balconies, 76, 86 n.9
ballistae, 53, 88
barbarian attacks, invasions, 52, 67, 87-100,
   106, 111 n.8
Barley, M. W., 43 n.21
barn at Verulamium, 97-8
barracks, re. Exeter 49
barter (*see* also markets, inflation), 89
Barton Farm, nr. Cirencester, Glos., 105
basilicae, Caerwent 95; Wroxeter 87
bastions, Chesterton (Water Newton) 25;
   Kenchester 26; Mildenhall 24; Thorpe 28-9
   (*see* also under town defences, late improve-
   ments)
Batava, Batavi, 72, 99
Bath (Aquae Sulis), rampart 62; Lansdown
   site 85, Fig. 17, Pl. X
baths, — houses, Catterick 96; Exeter 51; Wall
   (Staffs.) 38, Fig. 6; Wroxeter 22, 35, 87, 94
Belgae (tribe) (*see* also Winchester), 31, 102,
   112 n.11 (5a)
Belgic, — influence on Britain, —*oppida*, 23,
   31, 101-2
Bibroci, 101
Biddle, M., 15
Birley, Professor Eric, 86 n.14
Bishops, Bishoprics, 100, 108
Bitterne (Clausentum), Hants., rampart 62.
Bituriges, 111 n.8
Bodunni, 103
Bodvoc, 102
Boon, G. C., 15, 30 n.7, 75 n.23, 95

114